Nothing New

Nothing New

Principles of Dating from the Book of Ruth

ZACH GARRISON

with Kylie Garrison

RESOURCE *Publications* • Eugene, Oregon

NOTHING NEW
Principles of Dating from the Book of Ruth

Resource Publications
An Imprint of Wipf and Stock Publishers
199 W. 8th Ave., Suite 3
Eugene, OR 97401

www.wipfandstock.com

PAPERBACK ISBN: 979-8-3852-7180-1
HARDCOVER ISBN: 979-8-3852-7181-8
EBOOK ISBN: 979-8-3852-7182-5

VERSION NUMBER 02/23/26

For my dad,
Who showed his kids what it meant
To love a wife well

For my wife
Who has been a light in my life
Since we met

And for my Savior
Who has given me both

"I never hoped to slip away in stealthy flight; fancy not that; nor did I ever hold out the marriage torch."

—Virgil, *Aeneid* Book IV

Contents

A Letter from Kylie | ix
Preface | xi
Introduction: Why Ruth | xiii
Acknowledgments | xv

Part One: What Is Dating Anyway?

1 Friend, Betrothed, or Spouse | 3
2 The Purpose of Dating | 8
3 When Am I Ready? | 15

Part Two: Being Single

4 The Joy of Singleness | 21
5 The Life God Has Called You to Live | 25

Part Three: Finding a Mate

6 The Purpose of Marriage: Sanctification | 35
7 I Like What I See | 41
8 Looking for Character | 49
9 A Quality Wife | 53
10 A Quality Husband | 59
11 Some Last Considerations | 67
12 You Don't Know Unless You Ask (Others) | 72
13 When You Know, You Know | 79

Part Four: Avoiding Brokenness

14 Acting Unmarried | 91
15 Physical Unmarriage | 97
16 Emotional Unmarriage | 102
17 Spiritual Unmarriage, Plus | 112
18 Pulling Back the Reins | 115
19 Shooting It Straight | 126
20 Trusting God for the Results | 133

Personal Workbook | 137
Bibliography | 145

A Letter from Kylie

As Zach states in the first chapter, the overwhelming evidence that, in part, brought this book to fruition will indeed be "cold water to the face" for those who have never stopped to ponder these upstream principles. But if you dare accept, I challenge you to ask our God to give you a humble and teachable heart as you read these words, and if you do, what you are about to read can instead become a "refreshing drink for your soul." Before embarking on a faith-filled adventure such as the one you are about to read, consider first if you are a man or woman committed to these two necessary things: seeking first the kingdom of God and his righteousness, and trusting God to bless you the way he deems best in his timing alone. Above all, no matter the outcome of reading this book, remember that "those who wait on the Lord will not be put to shame."

Kylie Garrison

Preface

One Sunday morning when I was seven, I got home from church with a crumpled, folded piece of paper in my pocket. As I stepped through the front door, I took out the paper and carefully unfolded it, preparing to read the perfectly crafted announcement I had worked on all morning. I tried in vain to steady my pounding heart. This was the moment—I would declare it to the world! Fueled by my inner self's need to share everything on my mind with anybody who would listen, I took a deep breath and read off the paper with gusto, "I love Haley! I am going to marry her when I grow up!"

Haley was a classmate and a friend who lived in our neighborhood, and my eight siblings quite rightly erupted in laughter at my unprompted declaration of love for her. But they didn't understand. She was the one! She was blonde and she was a female and we were friends and . . . what else mattered? I did not know it, but this would be the first of many misadventures in my romantic life.

Ever since I was little (seven, at the latest), I knew I wanted to get married one day. I enjoyed thinking about the family I would have and the kids I would play with. In retrospect, *knowing* I wanted to be married helped me exactly *zilch* in figuring out how to navigate relationships with girls. So, in the middle school lunchroom, the time my jaw literally dropped while I stared into the eyes of a girl positively radiating with unforeseen attractiveness, I didn't have the sense to look away for the awkward ten seconds she stared back at me with a questioning look on her face. Knowing I wanted to be married one day did not save me, either, from the sheer panic that overcame me in seventh grade, when one of my friends informed me, "My ex is going to ask you out." *That* was an uncharted sea I had no idea how to swim in. Luckily, she never did get around to asking.

As I grew in wisdom and stature, I learned how to get "flirty." You know, reciting verses from Song of Solomon to the girls in my youth group (just the appropriate ones, Mom, I promise), charming the ladies with my hilarious teenage boy humor, and making smooth moves to ask girls to Homecoming (always ending with me in the Friend Zone).

My understanding of my romantic ambitions also didn't help when I finally did land a girlfriend in tenth grade. She was pretty great. We held hands. Then we broke up a month later.

In college, I would date two more girls, one before becoming a Christian and one after. I got engaged to the second girl. Two months later, the relationship ended.

As I grew, so did the consequences of my romantic misadventures, and my romantic inclination was not enough to avoid hurt and heartbreak. It was at this point that I wanted to understand: how does *God* want me to date? Surely, his way wouldn't cause so much regret and scarring. I set out to discover the answer.

It was in this search that God led me to the book of Ruth. And it was the principles he showed me there that I put into practice when I met my wife, Kylie. She, of course, had been on her own journey—recounted to some degree in this book. Not only did these principles "work" for us, but they helped establish the strong, loving marriage that continues to grow and nurture us today. It is these principles from Ruth that we credit with the success of our marriage, and it is these principles that this book will convey to you—so that you may know the joy of biblical dating, as we do.

Zach Garrison
January 2026

Introduction

Why Ruth

MANY CHRISTIANS LAMENT THAT the Bible says nothing about dating. And for the most part, they are right to think so. The closest we usually get to dating is a story like Isaac and Rebekah's: Abraham's servant sees Rebekah, he quickly claims her as the one for Isaac, she agrees to marry Isaac, they go back to Canaan, Isaac brings her into the tent, and *boom*, they are *married*.

That's pretty much how biblical relationships go . . . except in the story of Boaz and Ruth. If you've read the book of Ruth, read on. If you haven't read the book of Ruth, put this book down, read it, and then come back. No, really, go ahead. It's only four chapters; eighty-five verses; a fifteen-minute read, tops. It'll be well worth your time.

* * *

Isn't it great? I mean, what's not to love? Ruth is *awesome*: what kind of girl passes up the opportunity to go home to her family in order to go to a country she has never set foot in . . . with her mother-in-law? Boaz is a *stud*, not to mention a little picture, as a kinsman redeemer, of what Jesus would later be like. (In ancient Israel, a kinsman redeemer would take care of struggling family members, like a widow, because, say, all the husbands in her family died.) The story is seven-year-old Zach's dream come true: she's working in his field; he sees her and is all, "Who's the new girl?"

They get flirty, they fall in love, they get married, and they live happily ever after. It's a lot more spiritual than that, but that's the gist of it.

Without doubt, it's wonderful, but it is also more. The book of Ruth is primarily about God's providence in the line of David (and therefore the line of Christ), but the reader who's looking for it will also see in the book of Ruth, more than anywhere else in the Bible, an example of two people going through the entire dating process. These two righteous people notice each other, they spend time together, they consider the match, and they end up getting married. Ruth, read in this light, becomes a field full of treasures, waiting for us to uncover its wisdom for dating. And so, though I will Ruthlessly incorporate science, studies, my own experience, logic, and other Scriptures throughout this book, my primary hope is that you will be blessed to find the treasures in Ruth's field, as I did.

Acknowledgments

FIRST AND FOREMOST, IT is only right to thank my gracious God, who has had abundant mercy on me. Words could never be enough. You are worthy of all honor and praise.

To my wife, who puts up with my propensity to leave my socks and your pens scattered about the house, thank you. I could not have written this book without your support, your feedback, your encouragement, your graciousness to let me work while you take care of four kids, and your reminders to just slow down and trust God. I will always "yq."

To my children, who make me laugh every day, I am grateful to be your daddy. Without you, this book would have been done much earlier, and I would have been much sadder for it.

To my parents, who have done more for me than I can wrap my mind around, thank you for always supporting me in my ventures, for encouraging me to pursue writing in lots of little ways you probably don't remember, and for being continual examples of sacrificial love to us all.

To *all* my school teachers, you have impacted me in untold ways. Whatever craft and clarity I have gained as a writer are the fruits of your good labor for my benefit. Thank you. In particular, Mrs. Peck, Mr. Langhorst, Mrs. Kelly, Frau Biermann, and Dr. Jones, I am so grateful to have been your student.

To the TA in my Intro to Film class at USC and my American Lit professor at Northwest, your going out of your way to affirm me in my writing meant a great deal to me. Sincerely, thank you.

To Jason Yarnell, who told me these principles of dating were worth sharing, thank you for your encouragement and for your role in my life.

To my old youth group, in more ways than one, this book is for you all.

To Heather Clevenger, Jake Gibler, and my brother Daniel, thank you for taking the time to read my first draft. This final draft is far better because of your help.

To my editor, Wendy, thank you for your aid beyond the call of duty.

To my pastors, your insight and intentionality have been a tremendous blessing to me, in this project and beyond. Thank you for your willingness to give this book such careful treatment. I thank God for you, and I am in your debt.

And finally, to George, Joe, Karlie, and all the team at Wipf and Stock, thank you for your patience as I fumbled through the publishing process. I am very grateful for your help bringing this book to the shelves.

PART ONE

What Is Dating Anyway?

1

Friend, Betrothed, or Spouse

As it has for the last six thousand plus years, the world continues to go gaga over the opposite sex. Everybody's talking about the girl they like or the boy they think is cute. Everyone wants to have a special someone. And everyone tries to forget the reality that most dating relationships they know of end in heartache.

Ecclesiastes tells us there's nothing new under the sun, and to me, the prime example of a relationship gone wrong comes from ancient history. Over two thousand years ago, the Roman author Virgil, quoted in this book's epigraph, tells the story of Aeneas, who, though he admittedly had some valid reasons for it, was a real jerk about breaking up with Dido. "Calm down," he says. "I was eventually gonna tell you I was leaving you forever, and it's not like we were *actually* married." Aeneas acts as if Dido was making too much of their relationship. But research tells us that a breakup can actually be *more* disruptive and disorienting than a divorce,[1] and we've all heard plenty of stories of their devastation. Indeed, because of Aeneas's abuse, Dido very disturbingly kills herself after Aeneas leaves her, while he sails on his merry way into the rest of his epic adventure.

1. Seraj et al., "Language Left Behind."

We know this kind of thing is possible, but here we go, swimming into the shark-infested waters of dating, hoping those heartbreak-fish won't bite. We take to the internet to date online, we conduct an ever-increasing amount of research on dating,[2] and we can't stop thinking about it: *Who am I gonna date? Who am I gonna date? Who am I gonna date?*

In the twenty-first century, a quarter of 12-year-olds are in a relationship.[3] People lose their virginity (at age 17.34) before they fall in love (at 17.47) or enter a "serious" dating relationship (at 18).[4] They go through romantic partners like candy on Halloween (the average relationship lasts five months for 12- to 13-year-olds and twenty months for 16- to 18-year-olds).[5] Half of American women live with their boyfriends before they get married.[6] If people do get married (on average, at age 28 or 29 for women and 30 or 31 for men[7]), it is usually after going through several or even dozens of romantic partners. The world calls this normal and even healthy.[8] I beg to differ. To put it bluntly, the system is about self-gratification at others' expense. You either get broken or callous in the process. Yes, in a world of "body counts" and prenups, one thing is clear: the secular world has *not* figured out how to have healthy, lasting romantic relationships.

Unfortunately, the church is also far from perfect. Most churchgoers would agree that the Bible condemns having sex outside marriage,[9] but avoiding that has largely become the sole standard. Dating is seen as a stepping stone to engagement and marriage, so that the level of intimacy rises very quickly upon entering a relationship. There is little intimacy in friendship with the opposite sex, but *way more* in dating—physically, emotionally, and

2. Han et al., "Decade of Love."
3. Meier and Allen, "Romantic Relationships."
4. Regan et al., "Gender, Ethnicity," 670.
5. Meier and Allen, "Romantic Relationships."
6. Wang and Parker, "Record Share of Americans Have Never Married," 1.
7. "Figure MS-2: Median Age at First Marriage: 1890 to Present."
8. Meier and Allen, "Romantic Relationships."
9. e.g., 1 Corinthians 7:2

even spiritually. When we stick to this low standard, we pay the price! We play around, we get attached, and when it turns out there is absolutely nothing we can do to keep our significant other in the relationship, we fall apart. Like our secular counterparts, we have not mastered these relationships.

Marriage is good, and relationships are good; the problem is that dating is usually not. Far too often, dating, even between Christians, leads to devastation like Dido's. The mess of relationships is nothing new, but by applying the wisdom of God's word and the lessons of experience, by his grace, we might just enjoy the fruit of dating without being crushed by it.

So, let's start at the beginning: What is dating? Better, what *should* dating be? For an answer worth counting on, we must first and foremost consider what the Bible has to say. God's word is a lamp for our feet and a light for our paths.[10] It is useful to equip us for every good work.[11] In it, God provides "everything we need for a godly life."[12] Our search must be rooted there.

Unfortunately, when you type "Bible passages about dating" into the internet, the result is something like "slim pickins." To tackle this question biblically, then, along with many of the questions in this book, we have to take a more roundabout approach. Rather than jumping straight to Ruth, let's start by trying to find a sort of biblical definition for "boyfriend" and "girlfriend." After reading through the Bible, you will find that all non-family members of the opposite sex fall into one of three categories: friend (because we are to love all people as our neighbors),[13] betrothed (engaged),[14] or spouse. There's no wiggle room and no category for boyfriends and girlfriends. The Bible sees people as either not married, about to be married, or actually married—never dating.

If we're sticking to the Bible, we should really consider which relationship category dating best fits into. The answer is obvious,

10. Psalm 119:105
11. 2 Timothy 3:16–17
12. 2 Peter 1:3
13. Luke 10:25–37
14. e.g., Matthew 1:18

and it is clear where boyfriends and girlfriends categorically fit. If the only categories in the Bible are "friend," "betrothed," and "spouse," biblically, a boyfriend or a girlfriend is a type of *friend*. They are not a spouse, and they are not "about to be" a spouse. They are a friend.

This feels foreign to us. Strange. Almost laughably so. "*Of course they aren't just friends!*" We are used to seeing boyfriends and girlfriends do things—*constantly* do things, mind you—that could hardly be described as "just friendly." For those reading who are married, you may even recall doing things while dating your spouse that were certainly more than "just friendly." At the least, boyfriends and girlfriends talk constantly! They hold hands! They kiss! Is this not more than friendship?

If we are serious about seeking God's best for us in dating, then this cold water to the face is exactly what we need. We need to rethink what we've always assumed about dating when the Bible is categorically different from our perspective. We do not need a nice, printable (and ultimately arbitrary) "The Do's and Don'ts of Dating" list. We need to humbly seek God's wise counsel for us in his word.

The intent of this book is to prove the hypothesis that dating is meant to be a form of friendship. As we will see, it is a special type of friendship and will be distinct from other friendships in your life, but it should be a friendship, nonetheless. The more I have honestly considered the possibility of this definition, the more I am convinced this is the wisest way to date.

I suspect that some of you want to put this book down right about now. You're thinking something along the lines of, "Me no likey." I dare you to finish it. To consider it fully and honestly first. And as we continue in this book, looking at the story of Ruth, where this principle seems to be borne out, and examining how this sort of mindset played out in mine and Kylie's relationship, we will discover the power of this ethic: the security it builds, the excitement it brings, and the relational strength it fosters. As we commence, we will see how this framework is at the heart of God's best for dating.

REFLECTION QUESTIONS

1. What is your previous dating experience? Has it been messy, or free from heartache and regret? Why?
2. Do you agree with the claim that the majority of dating relationships, secular and Christian, are unhealthy? Why or why not?
3. What is your initial reaction to the claim that dating is meant to be a form of friendship?

2

The Purpose of Dating

RESEARCH SHOWS THE AVERAGE American goes on their first date between ages 15 and 16,[1] with a good chunk dating as early as 12, or even younger.[2] This means that most Americans date before they drive. Why? Why do people get into relationships so young? Why are people so eager to get into a relationship that will almost certainly end within a year or two? What is the purpose of their dating, and what should it be?

We can look to several different places to try to answer these questions. Let's turn first to research. One Pew Research poll illustrates that 40 percent of people are open to or seeking relationships that are more "casual" than "committed." In other words, it does not seem that many people date to try to make the relationship work long term. Tellingly, many of the questions from the poll were about physicality in relationships.[3] Putting the facts together, it would seem that many people date for the physical pleasure of it.

The poll further reveals that some people date simply *to be with someone*. It is interesting to note the type of someone people

1. Regan et al., "Gender, Ethnicity," 670.
2. Meier and Allen, "Romantic Relationships."
3. Brown, "Nearly Half of U.S. Adults Say Dating Has Gotten Harder," 1.

want to be with: for late-teens and those older, politics, already having children, debt, and, most importantly, living far away were of primary importance.[4] According to this poll, people date to be with people they can get along with and who will not cause them to sacrifice unduly.

Some professional psychologists say that we date because of our need for companionship; our drive to reproduce; our desire for love, intimacy, and security; and our desire to be taken care of and to take care of another.[5]

Popular psychology has its own views as well. One *Psychology Today* article confidently asserts that we date because we want to find our fellow dysfunctional *Prince Charming* or *Cinderella*, even if we don't marry them.[6]

Even "Christian" sites will advocate for dating as a way to have fun, develop social skills, learn about yourself, experience intimacy, and develop know-how for marriage.[7]

In all of these views, dating is seen mainly as an enjoyable, healthy outlet for human needs. Analyzing these views further leads us to see in them three primary categories of reasons people date: for fun, for pleasure, and for practice. Wisdom and reason will affirm the inferiority of all three.

DATING FOR FUN

Some people say they date for fun. It's not necessarily about the physical aspects of relationships or about commitment; it's just nice to have someone to be with—to spend time with and watch movies with and eat food with. And the question may well come up: what's the harm? Why not date for fun?

At first, this reasoning seems hard to combat. Given some thought, however, there are two major problems with it. First,

4. Brown, "Nearly Half of U.S. Adults Say Dating Has Gotten Harder," 1.
5. Meier and Allen, "Romantic Relationships."
6. Baratta, "Why You Date Someone."
7. Smalley, "Eight Great Reasons to Date."

nobody dates *just* for fun. In reality, fun is an *aspect* of dating, but never the central purpose. We go to amusement parks for fun; we play checkers for fun; we date people for other reasons. And even if those reasons are that you *like* them and want to spend time with them, the relationship is no longer solely about having fun.

If there *were* a hypothetical dating relationship that really was just about fun, there would still be a second issue. The problem, in this case, is seen when we turn the question of "Why not?" on its head: truly, what's the gain? As Christians, we often build our theologies and doctrines to justify doing the things we want to do; "*I like this thing, the Bible doesn't address it specifically, and, therefore, God must be okay with it.*" There are a million things that Scripture does not address directly. The Bible doesn't talk about fast food, but that doesn't mean you should eat it every day. The Bible doesn't talk about the internet, but that doesn't mean there aren't things to avoid online.

Rather than asking about the harm, we ought to ask what is beneficial and constructive about dating for fun. Ultimately, the gain comes from having a friend. A friend is a great gift from the Lord—someone to spend time with and watch movies with and eat with! But why does that friend need to be of the opposite sex in the form of a boyfriend or girlfriend? Why take it to that level? And if fun is all there is to it, then why choose this path of temptation, misunderstanding, and attachment that is guaranteed to come because one of you develops serious feelings for the other?

A relationship is meant to be a sweet stream of blessing in your life, not a shallow puddle of "just for fun," and not an ocean of tension because you refuse to admit that there is more than just fun involved. To put it plainly, saying you date for fun is either untrue or unwise: there is either more to it or there should be.

DATING FOR PLEASURE

Perhaps dating is simply a way to experience pleasure. Especially in today's society, pleasure seems to be the driving force to find a significant other. For argument's sake, we could assume that this is not purely about sex. As I've said before, God's word is clear: sex outside of marriage is wrong. But what about dating for pleasure *besides* sex? Is there other pleasure, perhaps non-sinful pleasure, that one can attain from dating? There is certainly pleasure in physical intimacy: holding hands, hugging, kissing on the cheeks and lips, and so on. I talked to one girl, a Christian girl, who openly told me her reason for dating was, "I just really like making out." The pleasure of intimacy is certainly real. There is also pleasure in staring into someone's eyes, in the butterflies that come in those moments, and in hearing someone say, "I love you." Should experiencing pleasure be our intended purpose for dating?

As we will see, Boaz and Ruth certainly did not date for pleasure, and there are *many* good reasons to follow their example. This topic will be more fully addressed starting in chapter 14, but for now, three points need to be made. First, any relationship that has pleasure as its purpose will end as soon as the pleasure fizzles. If one chooses to stick around in a relationship when it is not purely pleasurable to do so, it reveals that pleasure was never the true purpose to begin with. This leads to the second point: anyone who has been in a long-term relationship knows instinctively that there *is* something more to the relationship than pleasure. Even if a relationship starts out because of pleasure, it is not really the purpose of a relationship for long. Finally, as a rule, actions of intimacy leave scars when a relationship ends.

Again, we'll take a deep dive into this point starting in chapter 14 and look at the science of it all, but doing things like holding hands, hugging, kissing, staring into each other's eyes, and romantically saying, "I love you," are actually all part of "two becoming one flesh,"[8] a process Scripture only ever describes as being for the context of the marriage relationship.[9] When these instances of "becoming one flesh" are part of a relationship outside of marriage, they always scar those involved when the relationship ends, whether those involved realize it fully or not. It's as if you start spreading peanut butter and jelly together on a sandwich, then

8. Genesis 2:24

9. e.g., Ephesians 5:28–31; see 1 Corinthians 6:15–16

stop before you finish and try to put everything back in the jars—it's messy, and you always end up with jelly in the peanut butter jar. Like dating for fun, dating for pleasure reveals itself to be either shallow or harmful, and an unwise foundation for someone who is seeking a truly healthy relationship.

DATING FOR PRACTICE

The last potential category offered by our data is dating for practice. Many a time, I've heard motivations for dating such as, "I want to be a good kisser when I meet 'the one,'" "I want to get good at being a boyfriend/girlfriend so I don't mess it up when I meet my future spouse," etc. These types of statements reveal that people are concerned about being "good enough" for their spouse when they meet them.

Reasons to reject dating for practice are, in part, the same as the reasons to reject dating for fun. When it comes to emotionally caring for others, is dating really the best context to "practice"? Why not "practice" in other relationships—by being a good son or daughter, a good friend, a good sibling, a good employee, a good follower of Christ? Certainly, this gives you all the practice you need to love your spouse when you meet him or her. And, again, practicing in non-romantic relationships avoids the pain of breakups and misunderstandings.

But wait, can this be right? Doesn't the quality of future relationships suffer because of dating inexperience? As indicated in one study, there is *no correlation* between the quantity of previous relationships and the quality of future relationships. In other words, having a lot of boyfriends or girlfriends *does not* make you a better boyfriend or girlfriend. What *does* affect relationships, the study indicates, is family life![10] Another study demonstrates that family of origin, and the health thereof, affects both the likelihood of a person to date and especially to be in a sexual relationship.[11]

10. Meier and Allen, "Romantic Relationships."

11. Ogan, "Role of Emotional Dysregulation."

This all shows that it is not *dating* practice that affects what happens in future relationships; it is *family* practice. Your *family* is where you need to focus if you want to be emotionally prepared to be a spouse.

What about practicing, you know, the *other stuff*? Again, we will revisit this topic starting in chapter 14 (what a chapter that will be), but perhaps a brief illustration from my life will help for the moment. My wife was not the first girl I kissed. I had "practiced" before. And so, the first time I kissed her, *I got it all wrong*. She didn't like the way I kissed! I had to *relearn* how to kiss in order to love my wife well. Any previous "practice" did not lead to me being "good enough" for Kylie; it led to only one thing: regret. I wished—and still wish—I had *never* kissed anyone else. The idea that we need to "practice" before we meet the one we will marry is not founded in truth. If anything, it is a way to make one *un*prepared for future relationships, not "good enough" for them. So, it seems, as was the case with dating for fun and for pleasure, dating for practice is not a good reason to date, either.

What then? What is the purpose of dating? If dating is not meant to be for fun, for pleasure, or for practice, then the only remaining option is that dating, as in the book of Ruth, is meant to be for marriage. Dating is meant to provide a way to tell if a guy is the one you want to have as your husband. It is meant to provide a way to know whether you want to spend the rest of your life with a girl as your wife. It is not a "stepping stone" toward marriage, so that you are "kind of married" while you date, but rather an intentional pursuit by two friends to see if marriage is fitting or not. If we want to avoid the pain and scars that come with foolishly dating for fun, for pleasure, or for practice, we need to see the sole purpose of dating as preparation for marriage—investigating to see if the man or woman of interest is fitting to make a permanent part of your life. With the evidence as witness, there is no other good purpose to date.

REFLECTION QUESTIONS

1. What do you think of the idea that having fun is not a good purpose for dating? Is a normal friendship really a better place to pursue this goal?
2. Consider relationships you have experienced or witnessed that are founded on pleasure. Do you agree that pleasure is an unwise foundation for a relationship? Why?
3. In what ways can family relationships prepare you for marriage?
4. What benefits, listed in this chapter and otherwise, might come with the decision to date for the purpose of marriage?

3

When Am I Ready?

IF DATING IS SOLELY intended to be a consideration of marriage, what does that imply about when you're ready to date? First of all, if you're young and your parents are not okay with you dating, then the question is irrelevant at the moment. "Children, obey your parents."[1] Don't date. But assuming that's not the case, the question stands. There are several ways to answer this question, but perhaps the best way is with a follow-up question: If dating is for the purpose of marriage, then why date before you are ready to be married? If you do not feel ready to commit to someone for life, what sense is there in dating them? If you weren't aware, marriage can also very, very quickly lead to children (ask me how I know). So, not only is it a question of committing to someone for life, but potentially having a baby with them sooner than you expect! I am not commenting on the idea of having children quickly in marriage here, but if you are not ready to be committed to someone to the point of having a child with them, then I would encourage you to reevaluate whether you should be dating at all.

Here's the problem: given enough thought, an honest person will admit to him or herself that dating before you're ready

1. Ephesians 6:1

for marriage is almost always for fun, pleasure, or practice. That makes dating before you're ready for marriage *foolish.*

"But," you might say, "I *do* want to marry them . . . just not yet." Perhaps you are too young for marriage, or old enough, but you don't feel quite ready. Maybe you have something you want to accomplish first. So, you plan to start dating this person, and in three years—or five, or more—when you are able or ready, then you will make them yours forever. I would argue that such an approach would still be a mistake.

Before you label this book as legalistic, let's be clear. Dating, at any age, is not a sin. You won't find a verse in the Bible that says, "Thou shalt not date until thou art 18." I cannot say that dating at the age of, say, 16 (or even 10!) is sinful. My parents started dating each other at ages 15 and 16, and they are still happily married forty-five years later. I cannot say dating young is sinful, but I will confidently say it is generally foolish. Why? Because, to harp on the theme again, what benefit comes from dating before you are ready for marriage?

Song of Solomon is a book primarily focused on marriage. There is a repeated refrain throughout the book: "Do not arouse or awaken love until it so desires."[2] The contexts of this repeated refrain are filled with the woman's overwhelming sense of longing for her current or soon-to-be husband (depending on which interpreter you ask). This is a woman, either married or about to be married, telling those who are not yet in that place to *wait*—to *not* stir up these passions until the time is right (that is, not until the time when they can actually consummate those desires).

The primary application of this refrain is to physical intimacy; however, further applications can easily be made. Love is a beautiful ball of fire fueled by intimacy on every level—not just physical, but emotional and spiritual. Emotional intimacy produces longings to fulfill desires with one's romantic partner just as much as, and maybe more than, physical intimacy does. The refrain of Song of Solomon bids us to *not* fuel this fire until it is time for it to grow! Fire is meant to grow quickly and shine brightly, not be "tamed"

2. Song of Solomon 2:7; 3:5; 8:4

and fight its own nature to burn with passion. Imagine thinking, "I am going to have a bonfire on July 4th, so I'd better get it started by Christmas! I'm sure I can keep it under control until the fireworks." It is foolish to make a spark until you are ready for the fireball.

So, let's say you meet that girl—or that guy—and they are lovely . . . but you are only fourteen. What should you do? Biblical wisdom dictates that you *wait* to date them. It is not a sin if you don't, but what gain is there in awakening a deep love for someone that you will have to try to control for four years? Wouldn't it be better to hang out with that guy in a group as a friend, like you might any other guy? Wouldn't it be better to get to know that girl without the weighty label of "girlfriend" on her? Might it be that waiting is actually God's best for you? I think the biblical answer is clearly yes. If you are not ready to walk down the aisle, you are not ready to date.

If you are in a position where you are not yet ready to marry, taking this approach is, on one hand, a blessing. You don't have to worry about the drama, the temptation, and the mess that almost always comes with dating young. On the other hand, this approach will be difficult and will require a very real trust in God. First of all, you have to delay fulfilling your desire to be with someone. You also have to trust that God will provide what you need in the meantime. But there's more: what if the person you thought you would marry ends up dating someone else because you didn't start dating them "in time"? What if he moves, or she goes to a different school? In all these cases, you must trust that God wants what's best for you even more than you do. Romans 8:32 tells us, "He who did not spare his own Son, but gave him up for us all—how will he not also, along with him, graciously give us all things?" God wants to bless you, and he knows best. He has a plan, and if his plan for you is that you marry that person, he will work out the details when you are seeking to walk in the wisdom of his word.

As a last note, dating only when you are ready for marriage does not mean that you will marry everyone you date. While dating, being a process of considering whether to commit to someone for life, is quite serious, it is not *that* serious. A dating relationship is two people saying, "I think that person there is neat-o, and I think they'd be a pretty good spouse for me," and then finding out if they're right. That's not a commitment. There's no expectation; there's only a question of investigation. While it is best to wait to date until you meet someone you can see yourself marrying in the near future, do not be surprised if you find out you don't actually want to marry them. Move on and wait patiently for God to give you the next candidate.

Maybe you don't agree with me. Maybe you think dating is not that big of a deal and there's no reason to wait. That's okay. Keep reading this book. Even if you don't change your mind, you'll gain a lot anyway. But maybe you do agree with me. Maybe you are convinced of what I've seen in Scripture, and you believe that the Bible is saying you shouldn't date yet. And if that's you, then perhaps you feel it—that feeling in the pit of your stomach. *If I'm supposed to wait to date until I find someone I can picture myself marrying in the near future, then that means, for now, I'm stuck being . . . single.*

REFLECTION QUESTIONS

1. What does it mean to be "ready for marriage"? Do you think you are ready?
2. In what ways have you experienced or witnessed the difficulty that comes with prematurely awoken love? Do the trusted adults in your life agree that it is best to avoid awakening love before its time?
3. Consider the exhortation to *not* date the person you think you want to marry if you're not ready for marriage. What truths about God would be helpful to keep in mind if someone wanted to accept this exhortation?
4. What do you think so far about this book's argument? What points do you agree or disagree with? Why?

PART TWO

Being Single

4

The Joy of Singleness

It's good to understand that not everybody is designed to be married. If you haven't before, take some time to study 1 Corinthians 7:7–9. In these verses, Paul makes an observation that God gives different gifts to different people: some the gift of marriage and some the gift of singleness. If you are reading this book, odds are you do not want to be single for the rest of your life. Maybe you are even in a relationship right now. Don't check out. Don't miss this: Paul calls singleness a *gift*. As in, "Merry Christmas! Here's your present: *One coupon for being single for life!*—Love, God." Paul is talking about the ability to be content in singleness, but the language of "gift" makes it clear that Paul sees singleness as a great *blessing*.

What's going on here? Before we look at Paul's reasoning for saying this, take a second to consider with me: being in a relationship is a lot like having a job in high school. Some jobs are awesome, and some jobs are terrible. Some jobs pay well, and some pay less than minimum wage. But all jobs get you money to spend . . . and take up a lot of your time. That's the deal. You can either have no job, no money, and lots of time, or you can have a job, have money, and have less time. So, which is better? Well, both have their perks, but one thing is certain: it is good to enjoy your time before you have a job. You could even say that *not* having a job is a *blessing.*

In a relationship, even if you're not obsessed with your romantic partner or committed to them for life, you will spend a lot of your time differently than you would otherwise. Manly men, you might find yourself spending time at the ballet or watching a tear-jerker (*guidelines on this to come later in the book). Girly girls, you might find yourself listening to conversations about sports, cars, and the Roman Empire. Everybody, you will find that you have less time for your former preferences. And this only increases if you get engaged, get married, and especially if you have kids.

What should we do if God gives us the *blessing* of singleness, either temporarily or for life? We should *enjoy it* to the glory of God! Enjoy your hobbies! Enjoy your friends! Enjoy your family! Enjoy all the things that God has given you time for because you are not in a relationship! A relationship, like a job, may well come. But it would be a waste to spend all your time in singleness doing nothing but *wishing* you weren't single. Take time to enjoy the blessing God has given.

Counting your blessings might be reason enough for you to rejoice, but later in 1 Corinthians 7, Paul talks about the blessings of singleness on a whole new level. In verses 25–35, Paul argues that it is not only a blessing to be single, but it is *best* to be single! He gives two basic reasons. First, "those who marry will face many troubles in this life, and I want to spare you this."[1] In context, this verse is clearly talking about the difficulty of having a spouse and/or children in troubled times; financial crises and threats of harm are simply more difficult with a spouse and children to consider. However, we can say with confidence that marriage comes with its fair share of hardship at any time.

Relationships are not all they're cracked up to be. Even if you find someone *amazing*, they are doubtless going to disappoint you. Your spouse is going to hurt you in some way. They are going to make your life more difficult. The Bible is not short on examples

1. v. 28

of these sorts of marriages.[2] In singleness, those problems simply don't exist in the same way. You might have relational difficulties with people, but you won't be stuck living with those people for the rest of your life. Relationships are difficult, and marriage is especially so. In all these ways, being single is, in a sense, *better*. It avoids the pain, the frustration, and the hurt that come from even the best committed relationship.

In no way is this to deter you from getting married one day. But hopefully it shatters your illusions if you're expecting to float merrily from one day to the next, with your spouse waking up singing every day, radiating with joy and fulfilling your every desire. It's just not like that. Marriage is still a very good gift, but *so is singleness*. And when it comes to experiencing trouble in this life, singleness might be *better*.

The second and more important reason Paul gives for the superiority of singleness is that the unmarried are concerned about the Lord's affairs, but the married are concerned about the Lord *and* their spouse.[3] A discussion of this warrants its own chapter, as it gets at our very reason for living. Before we move on, though, a point should be made about the reality of singleness.

It is good not to waste your singleness being upset about the season God has given you, but maybe you *know* that God has designed you to get married. Maybe you desire marriage and you have been single for a long time. Some people are single for years, even decades, before they get married, and they *struggle* to be content in their season of singleness. If that rings true for you, know this: God knows your longings. He knows your needs. If you are asking him for marriage, he will not give you a snake.[4] Though Adam had perfect communion with God, God still saw his need for Eve.[5] Though your spouse will never complete you in an ultimate sense, there is a legitimate sadness that comes with longing

2. See Genesis 3:6, 12; 12:10–15; 20:1–2; 26:7; 1 Samuel 25:2–42; 2 Samuel 6:20–23; Job 2:9–10

3. vv. 32–34

4. Matthew 7:7–11

5. Genesis 2:18, 21–22

for marriage as a single person. It is not wrong for you to continue desiring and praying for marriage.

Of course, we have quite a Savior. And as you wait for his timing, you can find much satisfaction in him. Colossians 2:10 tells us, "In Christ you have been brought to fullness." Whether single or married, *he* is the one who can give satisfaction to your soul. A spouse can bring romantic intimacy, children, and other blessings, but Scripture assures us that *Christ* is the one who can make us content.[6] For eternity, we will not be married to our spouses,[7] but united with *Christ*.[8] We certainly need other people in our lives—after all, we are designed to live in community[9]—but we shouldn't view a future spouse as the answer to our problems, the prerequisite to our happiness, or the fulfillment of all our desires. Be careful not to let a romantic relationship become an idol that robs you of experiencing the joy of singleness that God wants you to have. Don't let it stop you from living the life God has called you to live.

REFLECTION QUESTIONS

1. What are the blessings of singleness, listed in this chapter and otherwise?
2. Read through the passages referenced in footnote 2. Based on these passages, what difficulties can come with intimate relationships?
3. How can someone be content in singleness? What does it look like to fully enjoy its blessing?

6. Philippians 4:11–13
7. Matthew 22:30
8. e.g., Revelation 19:7–9
9. See Genesis 2:18

5

The Life God Has Called You to Live

LAST CHAPTER, WE TALKED about Paul's claim that being single is superior to being in a relationship. The first reason Paul says this is that single people avoid the troubles that married people have in life. The second reason is that single people get to be concerned about the Lord's affairs alone. This brings us to the very purpose of our lives.

What are we here for? Are we alive to have fun, get married, have babies, retire, play golf, get dentures, then die? Paul seems to think the purpose of our lives is something more: to be about the Lord's business. Scripture supports this assertion in a number of places. First Corinthians 10:31 makes clear that God's glory should be the primary concern in all our actions. Revelation 4:11 tells us God is worthy of all glory because he created all things. Romans 11:36 states emphatically, "From him and through him and for him are all things. To him be the glory forever! Amen." According to Scripture, we are here for God's glory. And the way we glorify God most is by living the way he has told us to live.

When Jesus was asked to state God's greatest command for our lives, he put it this way: "'Love the Lord your God with all your heart and with all your soul and with all your mind' . . . And . . . 'Love your neighbor as yourself.'"[1] That means our focus in singleness *and* in marriage should be loving God and loving others. What does this look like?

If you are attentive as you read Scripture, you'll see that God's will is for you to love him and others consistently, though not exclusively, in a local gathering of believers—a healthy church. Scripture attests loudly to the fact that we need the church in our lives.[2] Committing to the church, regularly attending gatherings, building relationships inside and outside of formal meetings, serving people in the church, seeking to know and be known by pastors—this is how we grow in our ability to love and practice obeying God's greatest commandments. You will never regret pouring yourself out in devotion to God and in service to a healthy local church.

Likewise, God has given us a mission to accomplish toward outsiders. Though we are to love believers in particular,[3] our love should not stop there. We are to go and proclaim the gospel of Christ to the people around us,[4] loving them as we love ourselves. As others see our love for each other and our love for them, they ought to know we are Christ's disciples.[5] As with loving God and loving the church, you will never regret pouring yourself out for this mission.

Returning to 1 Corinthians 7, Paul is saying it is often *easier*, in a sense, to do all of this loving as a single person than as a person in a relationship. Although, as I've stated, I believe a boyfriend or girlfriend should ultimately be a type of friend to the other, there will naturally be more time, energy, and care spent toward that person than toward others. It is easy to put off building relationships with unbelievers, for example, because you think you should spend time with the person you might marry. If you get married, there will be an *obligation* to spend that time with your spouse. And if you have children, you will likely have very limited time to devote to other people and things.

1. Matthew 22:37, 39
2. See, e.g., Romans 12:3–13; 1 Corinthians 12:4–30
3. See, e.g., Galatians 6:10
4. Matthew 28:18–20
5. John 13:35; Romans 12:17–21

A single person has no such concerns. If loving God and loving others looks like jumping on a plane for a six-month mission trip, a single person can! If it looks like staying up late into the night to listen to a friend's problems, there is much less pulling a single person away from that opportunity. If it looks like being a friend to someone who is struggling with being single, a single person is uniquely equipped to love their friend through that.

God can and will use a single person in a way that a person in a relationship will either be hindered in doing (because of their desires toward their significant other) or completely unable to do (because of their necessary priorities). When it comes to serving God unhindered, to put it simply, singleness rocks! It is for this reason, Jesus says, that some people *choose* to be single.[6] In his words, they do it "for the sake of the kingdom of heaven." They do it because there is great power and great opportunity in singleness. That is part of the blessing of it.

We are all living toward a day when every knee will bow and every tongue will confess that Jesus is Lord.[7] We will all stand before the judgment seat of Christ in one of four states: We may come as one who does not know God or obey his gospel, earning "everlasting destruction."[8] We may come claiming to be a Christian but failing to have done God's will, earning the words, "I never knew you; depart from me."[9] We may come "smelling like smoke," having personally escaped the fires of hell, but "suffering loss" because of the poor quality of our work on earth.[10] Or we may come having lived a life after God's own heart, receiving eternal rewards, and hearing the words, "Well done, good and faithful servant."[11] In the moment of your verdict, I guarantee it won't matter whether you were ever married or not. All that will matter will be what you did with the time God gave you. Whether we get married or not,

6. Matthew 19:12
7. Philippians 2:9–11
8. 2 Thessalonians 1:8–9
9. Matthew 7:21–23 (ESV)
10. See 1 Corinthians 3:12–15
11. Matthew 25:20–21

we should live life to the fullest *for God*. We should make the most of every opportunity he gives us to love him and love others.[12]

As we have now established much of the biblical framework for dating and singleness, it is time we turn to the example of our favorite dating couple from God's word. Both Boaz and Ruth understood that God's call on their life was much more than finding a spouse. Ruth especially epitomizes a life centered around loving God and loving others. In her story, we learn that when she was married to Naomi's son, she treated Naomi with "kindness."[13] Later, when she became a widowed woman with an opportunity to choose the comfort of her hometown and a potential to marry, she chose instead to love the woman that God had put in her life. When Naomi urged her to go back to her family, she refused! "Where you go I will go, and where you stay I will stay. Your people will be my people and your God my God. Where you die I will die, and there I will be buried. May the LORD deal with me, be it ever so severely, if even death separates you and me."[14]

Two observations should be made from these verses. First, Ruth was loving Naomi in a way that *cost* her something. She was giving up a life of probable comfort and familiarity to go with Naomi to a country she had never been and scrounge for food. Ruth's decision was especially sacrificial because, in ancient times, it would be nothing short of emotional trauma to consider being buried away from one's family.[15] In short, she was choosing to *love her neighbor as herself*, no matter the cost. Second, not only was Ruth loving Naomi, but she was also choosing to love God! By choosing to go to Israel, Ruth was abandoning the gods of her fathers and choosing to serve the one and true God—*loving the Lord with all she was*!

Looking into the text a little further, Ruth's righteous character goes off the charts. Ruth 1:14 says that, after Naomi encouraged her daughters-in-law to go back home, Ruth "clung" to her. The

12. See Ephesians 5:16
13. Ruth 1:8
14. Ruth 1:16–17
15. Keener and Walton, NKJV Cultural Backgrounds Study Bible, 472.

Hebrew word for "clung" here is *dabaq,* the same word used in Genesis 2:24: "Therefore a man shall leave his father and his mother and *dabaq* to his wife, and they shall become one flesh" (ESV). Rather than "clinging" to a husband, Ruth "clung" to Naomi. She put Naomi's needs and desires above her own and made Naomi her priority rather than finding a husband. Later, in verse 16, when she says, "Your people will be my people and your God my God," it recalls God's central covenant promise with Israel: "I will be your God, and you will be my people."[16] Thus, Ruth demonstrated her love for Naomi like God himself demonstrates his love for us. To finish, she then proved her devotion to the Lord by swearing by his holy name, "Yahweh."[17] Before Boaz ever came into the picture, Ruth was loving God and loving others with her all. She was not wasting the singleness God had given her.

Though the story reveals little about Boaz prior to the relationship, we have enough to know that he, too, was loving God and loving others. We are introduced to Boaz in Ruth 2:1, where he is called a man "of standing," from the Hebrew word *hayil,* a term that connotes character, wealth, position, or strength.[18] (The same word is actually said of Ruth later, in 3:11). From that point on, the book of Ruth consistently portrays him as honorable and kind, blessing others in the name of the Lord.[19] So Boaz, too, was not wasting his singleness.

Boaz and Ruth both got it right in singleness. But their righteousness did not fall off when they continued into the budding of their relationship. In Ruth 2:13, for instance, Ruth speaks humbly and graciously, and it is evident that Boaz had been most kind to her in his speech as well: "'May I continue to find favor in your eyes, my lord,' she said. 'You have put me at ease by speaking kindly to your servant.'" Boaz then provides the hard-working woman with food and refreshment in 2:14, and later, in 3:5–6, when Naomi comes up with a plan to get Boaz and Ruth hitched

16. See, e.g., Exodus 6:7
17. Ruth 1:17; see ESV Study Bible, 479.
18. ESV Study Bible, 479.
19. e.g., Ruth 2:4

(we'll explore the morality of that plan in, you guessed it, chapter 14), Ruth follows through with her promise, demonstrating she is a woman of her word. Finally, in 3:15–17, Boaz makes it a point to provide food for both Ruth *and* Naomi—he doesn't only care about his love interest!

It is refreshing to know Boaz and Ruth loved each other well (as friends) in the context of a "dating" relationship, but it is clear that this wasn't a front. They had been loving God and loving others as a way of life—not as a way to impress a potential spouse, but because they were devoted to living life for God's glory. Boaz and Ruth understood that life was about much more than finding a spouse. It was about being satisfied in living for the one who made them.

Can you say the same? You are likely reading this book because you want to be in a relationship, now or someday. Is this desire overshadowing your desire for God? Is he the one satisfying you, regardless of your relationship status? Are you loving him with your all and loving others as yourself? Are you living boldly for Jesus, longing for the day when you will see him face-to-face?

The next section of this book will cover the process of dating and what it looks like to search for a mate. You'll also start hearing about mine and Kylie's story. But before you move on, I encourage you to spend some time considering your relationship with God, and how, like Boaz and Ruth, you might make it a priority above everything else. If you are single, don't waste your singleness. Don't wait to live the life God has called you to live.

REFLECTION QUESTIONS

1. What examples do you know of a single person loving God and others well in their singleness?
2. This chapter focuses a great deal on living a life of love toward God, the church, and others. How are you doing in each of these areas?
3. What details from Boaz's and Ruth's examples are particularly helpful or inspiring to you?

4. In what ways is loving God and others foundational for a healthy dating relationship?
5. Spend some time working through each question in the second-to-last paragraph of this chapter.

PART THREE

Finding a Mate

6

The Purpose of Marriage

Sanctification

THE TIME HAS COME: You are living the life you have been called to live—loving God and loving others. You feel you are in a place where you could actually marry someone—but who? What kind of person should you look for? And how do you know if they are really the one you want to marry? The purpose of this part of the book is to help you in your quest.

The answers to the question of what you should look for in a spouse start with a different question: "What is God's purpose for marriage?" First Thessalonians 5:23 says, "May God himself, the God of peace, *sanctify* you through and through. May your whole spirit, soul and body be kept blameless at the coming of our Lord Jesus Christ" (emphasis mine). It is clear throughout all of Scripture that, though we are counted as blameless in Christ, one of God's priorities in our lives is to *make* us blameless—to *sanctify* us, a word that essentially means "to make us more like Jesus." God wants to use the various relationships and situations in your life to mold you into someone who is like his Son. If and when you get married, he will want to use your marriage in the same way.

When considering whether to date someone, the first thing you need to concern yourself with is whether that person will help you become more like Christ. Second Corinthians 6:14 tells us, "Do not be yoked together with unbelievers." The image here is of animals hooked together on a yoke to plow a field. Imagine your spouse is an unbeliever: at best, that would be like one ox driving the plow crooked; at worst, it would be like having one ox hooked up backward! Believers and unbelievers are not concerned with the same thing. Your spouse may be generous, kind, polite, and charming, but they will *not* share your number one concern—to love God with all your heart—if they are not saved. While you desire to go to church, learn more about God, and give more and more of yourself to him, your spouse will *not*.

This may still be the case if you find someone who is "religious," "spiritual," or even "Christian." Many people enter into relationships and marriages assuming that if a person *seems* religious, and maybe even *calls* him or herself a Christian, then everything's peachy. And they spend their whole marriage frustrated, trying to get their spouse to go to church or be more God-focused, and eventually wonder if their spouse is saved at all. Don't fall into this trap. Before you marry someone, make sure there is evidence of sincere salvation; make sure you are pulling the plow in the same direction.

Though Paul's specific instructions end there, it is helpful to think of related wise principles as well. Think of marriage as a three-legged race. In a three-legged race, the ideal partners will have similar heights and speeds. If one partner is much taller and faster than the other, the two will move forward, but not as efficiently as if they were each with an appropriate partner. So it is with marriage. Maybe your potential spouse is genuinely saved, and they truly care about Jesus, but there is clearly a large gap between you two in terms of spiritual maturity. You are ready to trust God with everything, you have no fear about the future, but they are not sure God will provide. They struggle with trusting God, they struggle with trusting people, they are immature in their faith. Could you marry them? Yes. Would it be a sin? No. Would it be wise and God's best for your life? Probably not. When two people are unequal in the "height" and "speed" of their faith, it is likely to be a hindrance to both of them. The stronger one will feel held back from what God has for them, and the weaker one will feel like they are not measuring up.

Think about the previous chapter in this book; if the person you are interested in is not interested in living their life for God and for others, they are not God's best for you. If marriage is in God's plan for you, then he has someone for you who will seek to love him with all that they are and, therefore, seek to love you as they love themself. Do not settle for someone who "seems religious." Go for the Jesus freak.

The ideal three-legged race partners will not only have similar heights and speeds, but a similar game plan. Imagine there are two racers, each about 5'10" and speedy, but one always starts on the left foot and rounds the cone clockwise; the other starts on the right and rounds the cone counterclockwise. Both racers have the same goal, but their strategies are completely different.

In the same way, two people may have the same desire, to love God with all that they are, but God may have given them different strategies. She is being called to work with kids in Africa, while he is being called to work with the homeless in downtown Detroit. She has a passion to be in a touring praise band, while he has a passion to have ten children and live on a farm. He wants to be a lawyer, and she wants to be a pastor's wife. The issue in all these potential relationships is that the two people truly love God, but they are not being called to do that in the same way.

When two people get married, they become one flesh. Their lives intertwine, their ministries overlap, and their goals cannot be truly separate for long. If you are interested in someone who feels God has a very different plan for their life than yours, then, though they may be a wonderful person, it is possible they are not a good race partner. Healthy partners will share heights, speeds, and strategies.

There are other considerations to be made when it comes to choosing a spouse. How does the person you are interested in feel about your family? How do they feel about your friends? How do they feel about the way you dress? Your hobbies? Your sense of humor? God has called each of us to be a unique portrait of himself. Part of pursuing God's will for your life is being that unique portrait. If the person you are interested in is hindering you from being who you truly are (as God has designed you), then they are pulling you in a different direction than you are meant to go. If they bring unneeded tension to the other relationships God has put in your life, then God has someone else in mind for you to marry. You need a partner who is *for you*, not against.

Of course, not all change is bad. God will use the people in our lives, especially those closest to us, to refine our patterns of dress, our hobbies, our humor, and our relationships. Wisdom will be needed to discern good change from unhealthy change, but be aware that unhealthy change is a real possibility. (We'll cover this in chapter 12, but this is a great area to ask a wise friend or counselor about while you date.)

A good pairing in a relationship, like a good pairing of yoked oxen or race partners, results in blessing for all involved. Consider the outcome of Boaz and Ruth's relationship. Boaz and Ruth were both passionate followers of God. They lived godly lives and desired to keep pulling their plow in that direction. When they started coming together, the result was great blessings! Boaz was a great blessing to Ruth in taking care of her in her need. Ruth was clearly a great blessing to Boaz in marrying him.[1] Their child was "a heritage from the Lord" for each of them.[2] But the blessing of their relationship also overflowed to others. Naomi was blessed by the relationship throughout the story,[3] perhaps most when it resulted in a child that "renewed" her life and "sustained" her in her old age.[4] Finally, their relationship continued a lineage that would later include King David,[5] the greatest king to sit on the throne in Israel, as well as Jesus himself.[6] So that's pretty cool. I mean, really, how many people can say, "The God-man is in my family line"?

1. Ruth 3:10
2. Psalm 127:3
3. e.g., Ruth 2:18
4. Ruth 4:14–16
5. Ruth 4:17
6. Matthew 1:1, 5

While Kylie and I haven't had any King Davids yet, we can see how God has blessed us and others through our relationship. For example, he blesses us and others through our working together in ministry, inside and outside of the church context, and he blesses us and others through our not-King-David-but-still-pretty-excellent children. Getting to this point meant intentionality while we courted (we called our initial relationship "courting" rather than "dating"). Kylie is very much against Halloween. When we were courting, I was for it. That was a non-negotiable for Kylie—it was something we had to talk through until we saw eye-to-eye on it.

At the time, I was convinced God was sending me to India to be a missionary. Kylie has never been able to physically handle that kind of heat. Again, this was something I had to talk to God about. What it looked like for me was saying, "God, she's amazing, but I'm not sure we're called to the same route. Change my heart or change her heart; otherwise I don't think I can stay in this relationship." Within the next two weeks, I was excited to pursue opportunities with the Nepalese in Missouri that I hadn't known of before.

Other differences came up, mostly in secondary doctrine and personal preferences, and for all of them we had to consider: is this a deal-breaker? Can I be who I am and do what God has called me to do if I marry a person with these differences? If this is a non-negotiable for them, and I don't share their belief or conviction, can I yield to their preference, or can I not? In short, we had to find out how we'd run together.

When you find someone who is equally yoked and a good three-legged race partner, you are guaranteed to have no problems in your marriage. Ha! Just kidding. Many marriages go through a "honeymoon period" in the first few years. We had our daughter literally nine months after we said, "I do." Pregnancy (and therefore our first year of marriage) was defined by discomfort, vomit, aches, and pains—and that was just from me! Our marriage was filled with moments when we realized just how sinful each other was. "*You're not the person I married*," is a thought every married person is *guaranteed* to have. Seeking someone who is a good partner does not mean finding someone who has "made it" in their journey to become like Jesus. They will not be perfect while dating, and they will certainly not be perfect in marriage. But they will be *seeking perfection.* They will sin, but they will seek the Lord with all their heart. They will be imperfect but truly seeking to love others as themself. I cannot imagine what marriage would be like if Kylie did not have those characteristics. She is as interested in growing in Christlikeness as I am. That is the kind of person you want to marry.

God blesses those who enter into wise relationships. Wise relationships are defined by two people who are equally yoked in their pursuit of God and good partners for the three-legged race of marriage: they are heading the same direction, at the same speed, with the same strategy. Make sure the person you are interested in loves Jesus more than anything else. And then make sure they are someone you want to run a three-legged race with for the rest of your life.

REFLECTION QUESTIONS

1. In your own words, define equal yoking. Why is it important for dating and marriage?
2. Why is it important to date someone whose faith is similar in strength to your own?
3. What issues and pursuits are you passionate about? Which are non-negotiable for you? Which could you disagree with your spouse about? Consider writing these down in your "List of Fifty-Seven" in the Personal Workbook in the back of this book.

7

I Like What I See

EQUAL YOKING AND SIMILARITY in racing qualities are essential to a strong relationship. The purpose of the next five chapters is to help you understand what specific kinds of things you should look for within that framework. We'll first cover what every person should look for in a spouse, then what gents should specifically look for in a wife, what ladies should specifically look for in a husband, and finally a couple important points to consider regarding the process.

Let's begin in the book of Ruth, at the moment just before Boaz and Ruth meet. I'll preface by asking you to consider something: Boaz and Ruth are two human beings; how likely is it for two non-robots to go from being casual acquaintances to eager fiancés to baby-making spouses in less than a day? It's easy to miss this, but I think there is very legitimate "falling in love" going on prior to the later events of the story. It starts in Ruth 2:5. Boaz has *just* gotten to the fields. He greets his workers; they greet him back—*BOOM!* He stops in his tracks. "Who's that over there?" he asks. "Who, that girl?" his overseer replies. "She's the girl from Moab everyone's been talking about." Boaz doesn't even respond. He walks straight up to Ruth and says, "Hey, I think it'd be best if you were here every day until we finish harvesting" (that is, the next two-and-a-half months).

Now look, I understand that Boaz is being a righteous man and a providential aid for Ruth and Naomi, but come on! I cannot accept that there isn't the faintest bit of attraction going on. "At mealtime," verse 14 tells us, "Boaz said to her, 'Come over here. Have some bread and dip it in the wine vinegar.'" Man, Boaz certainly likes Ruth being close, doesn't he?

I suspect someone might think I'm reading too much into the text here. And maybe they're right. But something about the way Ruth talks to Naomi after meeting Boaz just has the ring of romance to it: "The name of the man I worked with today is Boaz . . . . He even said to me, 'Stay with my workers until they finish harvesting all my grain.'"[1] Ladies, if a man treated you in this way and took special interest in you all day, and you were recalling it to your mom, what are the odds that you wouldn't feel *something* for him while you told her? It seems to me this reading is confirmed in 3:1–4, when Naomi tells Ruth, "Let's see if we can get you and Boaz hitched," (that's the gist of what she's saying), and Ruth's response is a very quick, "I like the sound of that."

The point I'm trying to make here is simple: I think Boaz and Ruth *liked* each other. You know—like, *liked* liked. I think Boaz thought Ruth was awesome—like *attractive* awesome. And I think Ruth thought the same of Boaz. I think the thing that marked the beginning of Boaz and Ruth's relationship was attraction.

Attraction is a funny thing. It just *draws* you to someone. I love telling the story of the first time I saw Kylie. I was in college, getting home late from playing soccer (to a house I was renting with some other guys), and this gorgeous young lady was sitting on our couch. And I thought, "*Wow. Who is that?*" I was *instantly* attracted.

God created this sensation as a blessed gift to humanity—*amen, hallelujah*. It is a feeling that can spark interest in someone you've never talked to, as well as a feeling that can overtake someone after they have known their spouse for fifty years. It is

1. Ruth 2:19, 21

wonderful, and it would be a shame to ignore its goodness. Attraction is good! And it is good to let all forms of attraction—physical, as well as emotional (concerning personality) and spiritual (concerning the quality of their faith)—play into your consideration of who you will marry.

Perhaps this seems like an obvious statement. After all, why would you date someone you weren't attracted to? But, you know, Christians have what I think is an unhealthy tendency to embrace exactly that kind of thing. It is often accompanied by a "God told me that . . . ." Hear me say, I believe God does speak to people today. But, and I say this carefully, God is not in the business of giving mediocre gifts. In Matthew 7:9–11, Jesus says, "Which of you, if your son asks for bread, will give him a stone? Or if he asks for a fish, will give him a snake? If you, then, though you are evil, know how to give good gifts to your children, how much more will your Father in heaven give good gifts to those who ask him!" If you ask God for a good husband, how could it be that he would say, "Here. You won't enjoy this one at all. He's all yours"?

In response to this, some people might be tempted to say, "Attractiveness isn't everything." I one hundred percent agree! In fact, I know of marriages that seem to have started *without* much attraction, and it's true: you can have a happy marriage simply by deciding to love each other anyway, and physical attraction *can* come as you become more emotionally attracted to someone. Attractiveness certainly isn't everything—*but it is something*. And if God is the best gift-giver ever, and he wants to satisfy your heart, why would you be afraid to ask for someone you really like? If you want a guy who's really funny, why not wait for someone who can really make you laugh? If you want a girl who plays guitar, why not ask God to give you one? When it comes to a spouse, don't be afraid to be a little picky! This is the person you will spend the rest of your life with. How great it will be if you actually really enjoy them!

My standards for what I wanted in a wife were few. I wanted someone who loved Jesus, who was interesting, who could hold a meaningful conversation (about something beyond pop culture and social media), who wasn't glued to her phone, who was lovely, physically attractive, and who liked having fun. If she liked the same kind of music that I did, that would be swell, too. Kylie's list was much longer. This next section is written by her.

* * *

My side of our love story began about a year before meeting Zach, when my desire for a godly marriage had been ignited. Having recently given my life to Jesus, everything I had understood about life was inevitably being turned upside-down, including the kind of husband I ought to be seeking. In order to steer my new longings in the right direction, God put two books in my path that I still highly recommend to all single ladies desiring to be married: *Passion and Purity: Learning to Bring Your Love Life Under Christ's Control* by Elisabeth Elliot and *Lady in Waiting: Becoming God's Best While Waiting for Mr. Right* by Jackie Kendall and Debby Jones. The two major conclusions I drew from these books were:

1. Be still! God did not need my help in searching for or persuading a man to love me. My only job was to be patient and grow in my faith and relationship with *him*, producing as much fruit as possible in preparation to become submissive to another imperfect saint.
2. Eliminate any boxed-in requirements in regard to "tall, dark, and brunette," with the expectation that God would deliver exceedingly abundantly more than I could ask or imagine.[2]

In the midst of reading said books, God also gave me an older sister in Christ who encouraged me to, without having anyone specific in mind, write out a letter to my potential future husband. This way, I would have non-negotiables in writing that would safeguard me from settling for anything less than God's best for me. As a writer myself, I needed a bulleted outline to work from, and this ultimately became the "famous" list of fifty-seven qualities that were desirable for my mate. The initial shock at that number is common, but

2. Ephesians 3:20

understand that this list was only a starting point with *desires*, not *necessities*. Every few months after that point, I would go through the list and reevaluate what was really needed for an enduring spouse. This whittled the list down from fifty-seven to forty-one and, ultimately, to seven qualities: sold out for Jesus, trustworthy, sincere, encouraging/supportive, kind, gentle, and cherished children (with the inclusion of my dog, of course). Even though I really wanted to marry a bearded soccer player who led worship, had a big family, liked math, would dance with me, and used the Oxford comma, to boot, I knew that these were silly requests to deem "necessary" (except the dancing—which, in retrospect, should've been included as an eighth quality). I still wrote them down anyway because our big God happens to be a fan of big faith!

So, as I sat in my bed brushing my long tendrils, waiting for my prince charming to come around . . . Oops, wrong story. I wasn't sitting around; I was becoming one of God's best while anticipating another of his best! I started serving in the church, surrounding myself with more Jesus-loving friends, instilling spiritual disciplines, relinquishing the sins of my past, learning homemaking skills, loving on children, and learning to enjoy vegetables as I hoped my future spouse would. I was finally becoming a desirable, equally yoked mate, myself. Most importantly, I was becoming the kind of daughter that God desired to use for his kingdom's sake, whether or not I ever married.

Sometime a while after I had written "the letter" to my future hunny, I was reading my Bible when the Holy Spirit piqued my interest during a phrase dealing with "one year." I had no idea what God was trying to tell me, but I supernaturally knew it had something to do with my future husband. So I pondered this thing in my heart and went on my merry way. A few months later, I sure was glad that I had that letter dated!

On April 23, 2017, exactly one year after writing that letter, my roommate and I were hanging out at her boyfriend's house so I could get to know him better. I had been having a grand ol' time but sure was ready to go to bed. My roommate asked for just a *little* bit more time, so I obliged. As 11:30 rolled around, thirty minutes before the new day began, in walked the uber-handsome missing roommate with soccer ball and cleats in hand. Unbeknownst to either of us, though maybe hoped for, that specific bearded soccer player who led worship, had a big family, liked math, was a fantastic dancer, and—wait for it—used the Oxford comma was soon going to be my husband. Fast fact: he ended up having every. single. quality on that list of fifty-seven. What a marvelous gift-giving and romance-loving God we serve!

Give him room to work out all things for your good so that your faith may grow in turn and bring him great glory. And while you are waiting for that potential day, my hope is that our love story is evidence that he does great things for his name's sake!

* * *

Zach again.

God loves to bless us with the desires of our hearts if we are willing to wait on and trust in him. Attraction will usually be the first thing that interests you in someone else. If the first thing you notice about a girl is that she's gorgeous, it's okay if that's the thing that interests you initially. If the first thing you notice about a boy is his grubby soccer cleats, it's okay to want to find out more because of that.

Attraction is a good and healthy gift. Be glad for it, and don't be afraid to make it a consideration. However, it is extremely important to understand two things: First, attraction can be a silly screening tool if you let it be. If you find the perfect male, but he's missing one of his toes, that's a silly thing to make into a deal breaker. Make sure your list describing compatibility doesn't have items that are ultimately irrelevant. Second, attraction may be what gets you interested in someone, but, for goodness' sake, don't let it be a main concern in finding a spouse.

First of all, finding a person attractive in no way guarantees they are marriage material. If what you like about your girlfriend is "She likes action movies!" but she also happens to be the kind of petty person who wants to argue about everything and nags you all the time, Proverbs says you'd be better off moving to the desert[3] or to the corner of your roof[4] than marrying her. If what you like about your boyfriend is "his big arms," get real. Your husband may have big arms, but if he never uses them to take out the trash, give you a back rub, or rock your newborn baby when she wakes up screaming in the middle of the night, you'll wish you had skipped the whole marriage thing and gotten a pet rock instead. Big arms and action movies aren't necessarily bad things, but they are bad things to focus on at the expense of more important considerations.

Another reason you shouldn't make attractiveness your main concern is that people change! Your spouse's hobbies, interests, and physique will change over time (all three definitely have for Kylie and me). They may change so much, in fact, that after a while, you may even feel like you are married to a stranger. In some ways, marriage naturally gets harder the longer it lasts. Research suggests that, on average, marital satisfaction reaches an all-time low ten years in.[5] It's imperative that you don't think marriage is about always "clicking" and being "in love" with your spouse. It's that kind of thinking that leads to so many divorces. No matter who you marry, one day you will realize that you don't have as much in common with them as you used to. God has planned it that way. Your job will be to love that person, not because of compatibility, but because of commitment! "I love you because I *choose* to." Getting you to the point where you can say that to another sinful saint is one of God's most beautiful gifts in marriage. (For more on the true nature of marriage, I highly recommend Tim Keller's *The Meaning of Marriage: Facing the Complexities of Commitment with the Wisdom of God*.)

When searching for a spouse, let attraction play its part, but focus on something far more important—something that will not change nearly as much as someone's interests, or even personality. Focus on something that tells you who a person will *always* be. As we are about to see in Boaz and Ruth's story, that something is *character*.

3. Proverbs 21:19

4. Proverbs 25:24

5. Bühler et al., "Development of Relationship Satisfaction."

REFLECTION QUESTION

1. What attractive qualities do you desire in a spouse? Which ones are negotiable? Which ones are non-negotiable? Which ones should you probably just let go of? Consider writing the ones that count in your "List of Fifty-Seven" in the back.

8

Looking for Character

When it comes to marriage, why is character so important? I've implied this several times throughout this book, but the Bible emphatically states that marriage is meant to be *for life*.[1] Though some Christians believe there are certain exceptions,[2] divorce is not really an option. Once you get married to someone, you're stuck with them, which means, while you're dating, you need to find out for *sure* that they are the type of person you want to be married to. In other words, you need to be sure they have good character.

Character is the primary consideration in the book of Ruth. In fact, little else is talked about concerning Ruth and Boaz. We can see that although Boaz was probably attracted to Ruth in other ways, it was her *character* that really drew him in. In fact, he makes it his central concern to know about *who Ruth is* prior to even approaching her. Ruth 2:5 demonstrates Boaz's attraction to Ruth, but it also demonstrates that he values her character. Rather than seeing a woman he is interested in and going to talk to her immediately, he finds out what kind of woman she is first: "Who does that young woman belong to?" In the rest of the story, Boaz

1. Mark 10:1–9
2. See Matthew 5:31–32; 1 Corinthians 7:12–16

continues his focus on Ruth's character. Ruth 2:11–12 tells us Boaz is greatly impressed by Ruth; he appreciates that she has loved Naomi so greatly and so sacrificially. His assessment is confirmed in 3:10 when he realizes that she has not gone after young stud muffins, but after him, an older man, comparatively. Clearly, she is not vain or immature, but a good and godly woman.

It is also clear that Ruth is impressed by Boaz's character: not his bulging biceps, but his generosity, kindness, and care.[3] The story revolves around telling the reader that Boaz has done much for Ruth and Naomi. He, too, is a truly good and godly man, and that is what is most important.

Before you date someone, and throughout the process of dating them, you ought to have the same primary consideration as Boaz and Ruth. "Is this person a truly *good* person in *God's* eyes? What is their character like?" *Those* are the questions that need to be answered most. When it comes to this sort of investigation, proof is in the pudding. Notice how Boaz and Ruth didn't waver in their righteousness. They consistently did the right thing. So it should be with the person you decide to marry. Don't waste time with someone who is "working on" their constant temper tantrums. They need time to mature and become who they need to be in Christ before they are ready for a relationship. If you see, at any point, that your girlfriend or boyfriend does not have a hint of the desirable kind of character we will cover in the rest of the chapter, it is best to just stop dating them. This is a far better course of action than staying in a relationship—or worse, getting married—and hoping and praying they change. People often don't. That is not God's best gift for you in a spouse.

So, what kind of character should someone you marry have? There are two general answers, and several answers that apply to husbands and wives specifically. We have established that our primary purpose on earth is to love God and love others. It stands to reason, then, that the most important quality is that your spouse is loving—toward you *and* others! First Corinthians 13:4–7 gives an excellent definition of what that means: they should be patient and

3. Ruth 2:10, 13, 19–21

kind; they should not be envious of you or others; they should not be boastful, arrogant, rude, self-seeking, or easily angered; they should not hold grudges; they should delight in truth and not evil; they should be protective of others in their life; they shouldn't have trust issues; they should have confidence that God is good at all times and in all things; and they shouldn't quit when things get hard. Someone who has all these qualities is someone who is truly loving. Your spouse will not have these qualities perfectly, but if they are seeking these qualities well, they are the kind of person you want as your spouse.

Another key indicator of a person's character is their actions specifically with members of the opposite sex, besides you. Boaz knew that Ruth hadn't been seeking marriage from any other man.[4] She was not a promiscuous woman. She was not a flirt. It is hard to say anything about Boaz's relationship history with confidence. It could be that Boaz was never in a relationship before Ruth (talk about waiting a long time for a wife!). It is more likely that he, being "older," was a widower. Either way, he certainly does not give the impression of being a flirt, either. It is essential to understand what your potential spouse is willing to do with or to members of the opposite sex. Are they willing to flirt with whomever?—what does that say about the kind of spouse they will be? Are they unrestrained in the way they look at or approach other members of the opposite sex?—how restrained will they be in marriage? Are they degrading or unloving or unkind to their parents?—what does that say about the kind of person they really are? What does that say about how they will treat you when they aren't attracted to you in the same way anymore? Be very wary of the person who treats you differently from how they treat other people. There is something amiss in their heart.

All people, males and females, need to investigate the character of someone before dating them and throughout the dating process with them. If they don't fit the bill before you are dating them, don't start! If you discover they don't fit the bill after you've started dating them, break it off! Generally, the questions to ask are, "Are

4. Ruth 3:10

they loving?" and "Besides me, how do they treat members of the opposite sex?" It is of the utmost importance that they pass these tests with flying colors.

Before you get nervous, let me reiterate that "flying colors" will look different for everyone. Let your standards be high, but realize that neither person in a relationship will be perfect till glory. These qualities and the qualities we will discuss in the coming chapters are essential to investigate, but they are not possible to perfect in this life. Determine "how much" of a quality you need to see. Avoid marrying someone who falls below those standards, and certainly avoid marrying anyone who has a complete lack in any of these areas.

REFLECTION QUESTIONS

1. Which facets of love do you think are most important and should you have the highest standards for? Which might you have more grace for?
2. It is easy to be outward-focused in a chapter about what to look for in a spouse. But remember, someone will be looking for those same qualities in *you*! Work through 1 Corinthians 13:4–7. Are you a loving person according to this list? What qualities of love do you need to grow in? Pray for God's help in this growth.
3. How do you treat members of the opposite sex, including siblings and parents? Is there anything you need to change in your behavior?

9

A Quality Wife

AN ABILITY TO LOVE well and an ability to treat other members of the opposite sex properly are important qualities for both genders. But there are also desirable characteristics that are unique to husbands and wives. In my experience, these are covered by talking about the husband's responsibilities and then the wife's. I think, though, in this case it will be helpful to have the ladies go first.

Though Ruth is the epitome of wife material, as we will see throughout this chapter, it is most helpful to see her as exemplifying the traits called for in other passages of Scripture. There are three primary places in Scripture that describe an ideal wife: Ephesians 5, 1 Peter 3, and the book of Proverbs (especially chapter 31). Ephesians 5:22–24 explains that a wife's role is to submit to her husband. First Peter 3:1 makes it clear that there are no caveats here! It doesn't matter if your husband is saved or not, which means it certainly doesn't matter if your husband is a "good leader" or not. As long as your husband is directing you toward something that is not sinful, Christ's will for your joy is that you submit to your husband's will. Wow! What a tall order!

Before we continue, it is helpful to understand *why* this is. Two parallels to this relationship might be helpful for you to consider. First, consider the ongoing parallel, outlined in Ephesians 5:23–32, of a husband's relationship with his wife and Christ's relationship with his church. A wife's submission to her husband allows others to see a picture both of Christ's greatness (because a wife is willing to submit to his mere *representative*) and Christ's loving leadership (hopefully exemplified by her husband's). Because a wife is called to submit, people are able to see a picture of how amazing Jesus must be.

Still, as any wife knows, her hubby ain't no Jesus. And anyway, the Bible is clear: men and women are equal.[1] Why should women have to be the ones to submit? Why not men? Or at least, why shouldn't men submit on Mondays, Wednesdays, and Fridays, and women get those days off? If you struggle with these kinds of thoughts, consider the parallel of the Trinity. In the Trinity, there are three Persons, each equal in greatness and glory. And though he is no lesser, Christ *willingly* submits to the Father.[2] How incredible! Though they are infinitely equal, he chooses submission.

As Christ submits to the Father, wives are called to submit to their husbands. What makes this difficult is that in the Trinity, there is not an ounce of sin in the mix, and in a marriage, there is hardly an ounce without it. A wife is a sinful creature choosing to submit to another sinful creature. Only God could make that one work out. But isn't that the point? When the world sees a wife willing to submit to her husband, regardless of how perfect he's not, it's *odd*. It stands out. It makes an impression. And, ultimately, the only explanation is Christ. He is the only way a woman could submit to her sinful husband joyfully. In more ways than one, to make him known is the purpose of submission, whether the husband *is* Christlike or *not*.

When a woman understands the purpose of submission, submitting to her husband is . . . well, still very hard. Gentlemen, is the girl you are interested in dating or marrying capable of such hard work? I mean, she has to submit to *you*. Remember, in considering this, that the call is for *wives* to submit to their *husbands*, not

1. e.g., Genesis 1:27; Galatians 3:28
2. e.g., Luke 22:42

for girlfriends to submit to their boyfriends or for all women to submit to all men, so you cannot and should not assess her ability to submit based on whether she submits to you now.

So, how can you know if she will as a wife? Let's take a clue from the book of Ruth here. We must make allowances for cultural differences, but Ruth appropriately humbles herself before Boaz, even before they are married. She "bow[s] down with her face to the ground" before him,[3] and she refers to him as her "lord" and herself as his "servant."[4] Though Ruth is not submitting to Boaz as a wife in these moments, Boaz could be pretty confident, based on those moments, that she would be able to.

As with Ruth, there will be hints of a girl's disposition in your relationship. How does she treat you when you try to make a decision? If she's belittling you or has an "I told you so" attitude when you make a mistake, that's a bad sign. More than that, you can see if a girl will submit to you as her husband by the way she treats the male authorities in her life, particularly her father. If she disrespects and doesn't listen to *him*, you are almost guaranteed she will do the same to you. At this point, she is called to submit to or, if she's older, at least respect her father. If she is not doing that well, it's not an issue with her dad; it's an issue with her heart.

Ability to submit is hugely important, but 1 Peter 3 adds another item to the "character requirements" list. Verses 3–5 describe an ideal wife as someone who is not preoccupied with her appearance. In modern terms, that means she isn't obsessed with her hair, makeup, or body. It's not necessarily that she doesn't do her hair, wear makeup, or try to stay in shape; it's that those things aren't her primary concerns. What is "of great worth" in God's sight (like the ointment "of great worth" that the woman used to anoint Jesus in Mark 14) is for a wife to have a gentle and quiet spirit. A gentle and quiet spirit is one that takes harsh words with humility and gentleness. It radiates and instills calmness and peace, not anger.[5] Gentlemen, does that describe your woman? Because the book of

3. Ruth 2:10
4. Ruth 2:13
5. Caffin, *Commentary on 1 Peter*, commentary on 1 Peter 3:4.

Ruth doesn't have a lot of harshness directed toward Ruth, we don't see this trait come out as I've described it here. But Ruth definitely exudes humility, as we've talked about above, and peace and blessing come to others because of her attitude and responses. Gentlemen, does that describe your woman? Does she make others walk on eggshells? Or does she ease the tension from situations? Is she a blessing in times of strife? If she is, she's a winner.

Verse 6 adds still another item to our list. An ideal wife is one who, like Sarah, "[does] not give way to fear." Various interpretations of this verse have been suggested, but the unifying element in all interpretations seems to be *toughness*. A wife, like Sarah, should be tough. She should rely on God's goodness and know that he is always near. In mentioning Sarah, the reader is also reminded of Sarah's life: picking up and following Abraham wherever he went; trusting her husband when he followed God, and trusting God when he didn't; and several times ending up in highly unfavorable situations by her husband's leadership, or lack thereof.[6] Sarah was able to endure all of this because she did not give way to fear. She trusted God and was therefore *tough*.

Some people think that girls should be small and frail and helpless. Sarah was not this way. She walked beside her man with strength. Of course, we could say the same thing about Ruth: she demonstrated her toughness by sticking with Naomi and working hard for their food, even in the midst of the grief of losing her husband. Gentlemen, can the girl you are interested in walk like these women?

Finally, Proverbs has something to say about the ideal wife. Earlier, I referenced two proverbs that compare living with a quarrelsome wife to living in a desert or on the corner of a rooftop. Being quarrelsome is something, girls, that you should certainly strive to avoid. However, our last passage, Proverbs 31, is chock full of many other attributes of a woman of "noble character."[7] To name a few, Proverbs 31 says a godly woman has developed skills, is able to contribute to the family's success, is knowledgeable, is

6. See Genesis 12:10–20; 20:1–18

7. Proverbs 31:10

hard-working, helps her husband succeed, and much, much more. Gentlemen, I would encourage you to search this Scripture passage thoroughly and ask yourself, "Does this describe the girl I'm interested in?" As with submission, the question is not necessarily, "Is she doing these things for me now?" but, "Is she the kind of woman that I could easily imagine doing these things?"

Keep in mind that the portrait of the woman in Proverbs 31 is intentionally painted with impossibly high standards. Based on the high similarity of language between the description of this woman in Proverbs 31 and the description of wisdom in action and even wisdom itself throughout Proverbs, we should see that this woman is essentially the idealized embodiment of wisdom.[8] Your wife will not do all of these things (or their modern equivalents) at all times in your marriage, but her character should be *like* the Proverbs 31 woman's—capable, industrious, generous, and wise. If you would like a realistic example of what that might look like, consider the Proverbs 31 woman named in this book's title. That's right, Ruth 3:11 calls Ruth a "woman of noble character," exactly like the "wife of noble character" that Proverbs 31 describes. (The Hebrew is actually identical in Ruth 3:11 and Proverbs 31:10—*'eshet khayil.*) If your wife is like the Proverbs 31 woman, or like Ruth, God has high praise for her indeed: like wisdom itself, "She is worth far more than rubies."[9]

Ladies, you have a very high calling. God is calling you to be a woman who can submit to and respect her husband, who cares much more about the state of her spirit than the appearance of her body, who is tough, who is not quarrelsome, who is skilled, who is knowledgeable, and who is able to help her family and husband succeed. In short, God is calling you to be like Ruth. This list of qualities is not exhaustive; if you are willing to take a deep dive into Scripture, you will discover even more.

8. Cf. 31:10 with 3:15 and 8:11; 31:14–15 with 6:8 and 30:25; 31:15–18 with 24:30–34; 31:20 with 14:31; 31:23 with 1:21 and 8:3; 31:25 with 1:26 and 8:30–31; 31:26 with e.g., 1:8, 3:1, 4:2, 6:20, and 13:14; 31:27 with 6:6 and 24:30; 31:30 with 1:7 and 9:10; and 31:31 with 8:19

9. Proverbs 31:10

So, are you up for the challenge of becoming a woman of noble character? Keep in mind two very important things. First, you will fail at this! You need Jesus to transform you, and you need his grace when you fall short. And ultimately, this is not a "character makeover to win a man." This is a character makeover for your eternal husband, Jesus. Christ wants to make you holy, as he is holy.[10] Rely on him to be the woman you were created to be.

Gentlemen, now you have an idea of what to look for. Will you settle for less? Will you compromise? Do not expect perfection; she will not be perfect at any of this and won't be until eternity. But she should be pulling her spiritual plow strongly in the right direction. You should have grace for her shortcomings, but if you have a very difficult time imagining her as a capable, godly woman, she is probably not the one for you. Wait for God's best, and don't settle for less.

REFLECTION QUESTIONS

1. Ladies, in which of the qualities mentioned in this chapter has God already grown you? Praise God for his work in your life, and pray that it would continue!
2. Ladies, in which areas do you most need to grow?
3. Gentlemen, which of the qualities mentioned in this chapter are most important to you? Which are negotiable, and which are non-negotiable? Consider adding these to your "List of Fifty-Seven" in the back of the book.
4. What qualities does other Scripture indicate a godly wife should have? Consider recording these insights in your "List of Bible Passages" in the back of the book.

10. 1 Peter 1:15–16

10

A Quality Husband

LIKE RUTH, BOAZ IS the epitome of marriage material. But here, too, we will approach his example via the exhortations of other passages. Scripture talks about the ideal husband in two primary places: Ephesians 5 and 1 Peter 3. Using these two passages, we can extrapolate many desirable qualities for an ideal husband so that we get a pretty complete picture.

Let's start with Paul's instructions to wives from Ephesians 5. If God has called the wife to submit to her husband, that means he has called the husband to be the leader of his wife, and therefore of the whole family. As we have discussed, this is a beautiful opportunity for those around the couple or family to see a picture of Christ's greatness. Ladies, as you work toward being able to submit to this man one day, consider how easy he will make it for you to do so. Is he the kind of man who will be easy to submit to? Will he be a good leader, like Boaz, who seems to command the respect of the city elders?[1] Or will he be a Nabal, forcing you, his wife, to clean up the mess he leads your family into?[2]

1. See Ruth 4:2
2. See 1 Samuel 25

Biblically, a good leader needs many qualities. More than anything, he needs to be wise. Wisdom is a grand virtue, with entire books of the Bible committed to its description—especially Proverbs, Ecclesiastes, Job, and James. If you want a full description of what a wise husband should look like, you could spend many hours looking in those books. (Again, space to record insights can be found in the workbook.) In terms of leadership, though, three qualities are especially important: humility, wisdom in choosing friends, and wisdom in speech.

We know a lot more about Ruth than Boaz, but Boaz seems to demonstrate real humility in the story. This is most clearly seen when Ruth approaches him at night, and Boaz says, "This kindness is greater than that which you showed earlier: You have not run after the younger men, whether rich or poor."[3] Boaz is not full of himself. He is genuinely humbled and blessed by her choosing him.

For younger husbands, especially, humility takes another very important form. Again and again, in various ways, Proverbs exhorts its readers to acquire many counselors. For example, Proverbs 15:22 says, "Plans fail for lack of counsel, but with many advisers they succeed."[4] Ladies, at the end of the day, your husband will be calling the shots. As we'll see, this doesn't mean that you can't give input. It does mean that God ultimately gives *him* the responsibility to make the final decision and will hold *him* accountable for it. He will likely be young and inexperienced in this kind of decision-making. If he is unable to ask for help from those older and wiser than him, he will lead your family down foolish paths. As Proverbs 11:2 says, "When pride comes, then comes disgrace, but with humility comes wisdom." Which part of that verse describes the gentleman you are interested in? Is he proud, or is he humble? Does he seek others for advice? When you are married, your husband will either make all the decisions without input, or he will value advice (including yours!). Maybe the gentleman you are interested in fancies himself an expert in certain things. Does

3. Ruth 3:10
4. See also Proverbs 11:14; 24:6

he consider a knowledgeable man's input anyway? If your husband is not at all humble, he will not be a good husband.

A husband needs to be able to ask for advice when he does not know what to do. He needs to understand that he desperately needs God's wisdom to lead his family well. He needs to be pursuing wisdom prior to and throughout marriage. One of the primary ways a man becomes wise is by associating with godly men. As Proverbs 13:20 says, "Walk with the wise and become wise, for a companion of fools suffers harm." Of course, Boaz seems to have surrounded himself with wise, trustworthy people,[5] but we see the ultimate example of "walking with the wise" in the training of the disciples of Jesus. Jesus picked as his apostles twelve rather unimpressive men, both morally and in regard to education. They are constantly getting things wrong throughout the Gospels. But look at the result of their spending time with the wisest person to ever walk the earth: "When they saw the courage of Peter and John and realized that they were unschooled, ordinary men, they were astonished and they took note that these men had *been with Jesus*" (emphasis mine).[6] We become like the company we keep. Our choice of friends says a lot about the kind of person we want to become. Ladies, what kind of people does the gentleman you are considering call his friends? Does he surround himself with wise brothers that he might gain from their wisdom? Or are his friends a bunch of losers who aren't going anywhere, especially spiritually? His selection of friends will tell you a lot about how interested he is in being a wise man of God.

Finally, a husband needs to be wise in his speech. Ephesians 4:29 exhorts, "Do not let any unwholesome talk come out of your mouths, but only what is helpful for building others up according to their needs, that it may benefit those who listen." James 1:19 adds, "Everyone should be quick to listen [and] slow to speak." Do these verses describe the gentleman you are interested in marrying? Does he speak with wisdom? This is an area where Boaz really shines. His words are full of grace and insight. "The Lord be with

5. See Ruth 2:6–7; 15–16; 4:2

6. Acts 4:13

you!" are the first words from his mouth in the story,[7] and his tone never deviates. Imagine a husband who is careless with his words. Or worse, a husband who won't listen to a word you say and constantly abuses you with his language. Is this the kind of leader you want for a husband? His mouth will get him into trouble with others, it will make his and your relationships with others suffer, and it will tear down his number one advisor at home: you! Do not marry a man who is utterly foolish—in his pride, in his choice of friends, or in his speech. He will make a poor leader, indeed.

One more quality of leadership bears mentioning. As we see in the example of Boaz, an effective leader, husband, and man, is decisive.[8] This trait is consistent in the other great leaders of Scripture as well. Nehemiah decides to stick to his task of building the wall when his enemies repeatedly invite him to talk.[9] The apostles decide to delegate responsibility when food needs to be equitably distributed to the church's widows.[10] Jesus decides to move on to the next town when the people try to get him to stay in Capernaum.[11] These men are *decisive*. They know what they are called to do, they decide what they think is the best option to accomplish their calling, and they do it.

There is nothing more ineffective than a leader who can't make up his mind. If you want a strong leader for a husband, he needs to be decisive.[12] That means, boys, if you are not a decisive person, start practicing: the next time someone asks what you want for dinner, come up with a real, reasonable answer—*not* "I don't know," and *not* "I don't care."

A man with all these qualities of leadership could still be a tyrant. He may be the kind of guy who dominates you and belittles you and doesn't value what you have to say. That is not the kind of

7. Ruth 2:4

8. See Ruth 2:8–9, 14–16; 3:11–15; 4:1–10

9. Nehemiah 6:1–4

10. Acts 6:2–4

11. Luke 4:42–44

12. I am indebted to Jason Yarnell for these insights on wisdom and leadership.

husband God wants you to have. Ephesians 5:25 says, "Husbands, love your wives, just as Christ loved the church and gave himself up for her." Husbands are to give themselves up for their wives, *just like* Christ gave himself up for the church. Like the task of a wife, this is a tall order! How did Jesus give himself up for the church? The first thing that comes to mind is probably by dying an excruciating death for it! A husband should be willing to take a bullet, a knife, a club, a punch, or abuse of any kind for his wife. He should be brave, protective, and full of sacrificial love to do this, as Christ was for his church. While this is extremely important, I think the bigger concern for a husband is emulating Christ in the *other* way he gave himself up for the church. As the apostle Paul would later emulate,[13] Christ died *every day* for his bride; every day in his ministry was an act of sacrificial love. Philippians 2:6–7 describes Christ's daily sacrifice like this: "Being in very nature God, [he] did not consider equality with God something to be used to his own advantage; rather, he made himself nothing by taking the very nature of a servant, being made in human likeness." Every single day of his ministry, God himself decided to not only live with the limitations of human existence, but to live alongside, love, and serve great sinners.

Several times in Scripture, we get a sense of the frustrations of this experience. Jesus talks to his disciples in a way that seems harsh, saying things like, "Do you still not understand?" or, "How long shall I put up with you?"[14] Jesus was not being sinful in these instances; he was reminding the disciples of the reality of his daily sacrifice in choosing to love and serve them. Jesus lived this way *every day*. The cross is the *culmination* of that love. Like Philippians 2:8 says, "And being found in appearance as a man, he humbled himself by becoming obedient to death—even death on a cross!" This is the way that a husband is to love his wife: choosing to sacrifice his time, energy, and comfort every day in order to love and serve her like Christ did his church. He should, like Christ, even be willing to take the job of the lowest servant, crawling on his knees

13. 1 Corinthians 15:31 (ESV); see also Luke 9:23

14. Matthew 16:9; 17:17

and washing the filth off the feet of the one he loves.[15] Ladies, does the gentleman you are interested in display the capacity for *this* kind of love? Will he love you enough to lead as a servant? Will he put your needs and the needs of your family above his own? Will he not only lead like Christ, but love like him? If you want God's best for you, he must be this type of man.

In addition to observing the *nature* of Christ's love for the church, Ephesians 5 also outlines the *aim* of Christ's love as a model for husbands. First, Christ concerns himself primarily with the spiritual needs of his church. He cleanses her "by the washing with water through the word."[16] We can apply this, also, to husbands. A husband is to concern himself with the spiritual needs of his wife. He is to seek out, as a first priority, ways to serve her so that she might grow closer to Christ. He is to take the kids so she can have time to read her Bible and pray. He is to provide and plan for her to go on weekend getaways with godly women. He is to read the Bible with her and pray with and for her.

In addition to her spiritual needs, he is to take care of his wife physically and emotionally, "feeding" and "caring" for her, according to verse 29. To this, 1 Peter 3:7 adds that he should understand his wife has needs that he doesn't have. He should respect her and recognize those needs. A godly husband should be willing to rub his wife's feet and neck. He should give her time to relax. He should listen to her when she talks. He should care about her challenges. Christ perfectly loved and continues to love the church in all these ways. Because, as we've established, your hubby won't be no Jesus, perhaps a lesser example will be helpful to provide as well. I am referring, of course, to Boaz. Repeatedly throughout the story, Boaz demonstrates that he will be one who provides for and cares for Ruth.[17] Ladies, find a man who will do the same for you. Find a man who will be a picture of Christ to you and to those around him.

The final character trait you need to look for in a husband is strength. Physical strength is good, but more important is that

15. John 13:1–17

16. v. 26

17. Ruth 2:8–9; Ruth 2:8, 9, 14, 15–16, 21; 3:15

a man is spiritually strong. A coward cannot effectively lead and love like Christ, and knowing what to do means nothing if a man does not have the strength to carry it out. When circumstances are difficult, a quality husband will not cower and will "not become weary in doing good," for he knows "at the proper time [he] will reap a harvest if [he does] not give up."[18] He is willing to follow through on the exhortation from 1 Corinthians 16:13. As stated in the ESV, "Be watchful, stand firm in the faith, act like men, be strong." As the leader of his house and as a man of God, a quality husband is fearless. He, like Boaz in the end of his story, works tirelessly to do all that God has called him to do.[19] He trusts in God, and he never gives up doing what he ought to. Ladies, is your interest such a man?

So that is our list. A godly man of the marrying type is a quality leader. He is humble, careful in his selection of friends, wise in speech, and decisive. He is willing to love his wife—sacrificially, spiritually, physically, and emotionally—and is spiritually strong. In short, he is not only like Boaz, but also like Christ. Keep in mind that this, too, is not an exhaustive list; there is more the Bible can tell you (workbook is in the back). And remember, as well, that he will not be perfect. He should not be devoid of these qualities, and he should always be seeking to improve, but have grace for his shortcomings, as he ought to have grace for yours.

Ladies and gentlemen alike, as you date, be sure to concern yourself primarily with the character qualities of the person you want to consider for marriage. Are they a godly, loving person? Do they seem like they will make a godly husband or wife? Secondarily, but also very important, do you enjoy them as a person? In the process of assessing whether they are equally yoked and a good three-legged race partner, *these* are the essential questions to answer.

One free tip before the next chapter: Although you should observe someone closely to know whether you want to marry them, know, too, that having a list of intentional questions to work through as you court is both helpful and fun. As a rule of thumb, I

18. Galatians 6:9

19. See Ruth 3:18

would advise getting to more personal and intimate questions only as the courtship progresses. Start with the less serious stuff: What are their hobbies, their interests, their likes and dislikes, their favorite books, movies, and places to go on vacation? Keep in mind that these conversations shouldn't be shallow. Investigating compatibility means finding out *why* they like the things they like and what kind of person they really are, not just that you have the same favorite color. Then move on to more serious stuff: Where do they see themself in ten years? Do they feel a specific calling from God toward anything? Continue to progress toward even more serious subjects: Have you had sexual sin in your life? What struggles do you have that might affect me if we get married? Is there anything that would make you a bad spouse? Sprinkle in some fun ones, but be sure to have these rich conversations about things that really matter.

REFLECTION QUESTIONS

1. Gentlemen, in which of the qualities mentioned in this chapter has God already grown you? Praise God for his work in your life, and pray that it would continue!
2. Gentlemen, in which areas do you most need to grow?
3. Ladies, which of the qualities mentioned in this chapter are most important to you? Which are negotiable, and which are non-negotiable? Consider adding these to your "List of Fifty-Seven" in the back of the book.
4. What qualities does other Scripture indicate a godly wife should have? Consider recording these insights in your "List of Bible Passages" in the back of the book.

11

Some Last Considerations

Before finishing up this section about qualities to look for, there are a few things that some people will need to hear. First and foremost, considering all the preceding qualities to value, it's worth mentioning the obvious: the best place to find a godly man or a godly woman is often in your local church. This will not happen all the time, but especially if your church is quite healthy, the odds are high that there is someone awesome and single around. My advice is to start in your spiritual home.

Next, earlier I mentioned people who get married without being very attracted to their spouse. I also mentioned that this decision is often accompanied by the line, "God told me that . . . ." I want to discuss this more fully before moving on to the next chapter. Christians who are especially eager to do God's will can find themselves considering marriage to someone whom they find incompatible, unequally yoked, or both. They maintain that sometimes God asks us to do things that we don't want to do. "His ways are not our ways!" they proclaim.[1] I know some Christians do this because I used to be one of them. As I stated in the preface, I was engaged to a girl before I met Kylie. Deep down, I knew I did

1. See Isaiah 55:8–9

not really want to marry her, but I thought, and even told her, that God had said we were going to be married. There lies a great danger in this way of thinking, especially when it comes to dating and marriage. "God told me that they will be my spouse" could be an absolutely terrible reason to marry someone. In my case, it caused great hurt for me and even greater hurt for my former fiancée. If you are in a similar situation, this section is for you.

If you believe God has told you that you will or should marry someone, I think it is wisest to take that experience as a *possible* indication or confirmation to continue your pursuit, but never as a foundational reason that you should actually marry that person. There are three reasons I say this. First, there is a biblical principle that what is *right* to do is also *pleasing* to do. God gives us verses like Proverbs 19:23, which says, "The fear of the LORD leads to life; then one rests content, untouched by trouble." That means when one follows God and is obedient to him, the result should be contentment and security, *not* apprehension. Psalm 37:4 famously exhorts, "Take delight in the LORD, and he will give you the desires of your heart." This means that when you are joyfully seeking Christ, God will increase your joy by fulfilling your God-honoring desires; he will not diminish your joy by asking you to do something dreadful.

I know what you're thinking: God asks us to do hard things all the time! You need only think of a story about a martyr to see that God will require "dreadful" experiences for some of his children. Remember, though, these experiences are not truly dreadful. The Bible again and again reveals that these trials are actually the places where we experience *real joy* in Christ![2] Consider Stephen as he was being killed: *filled* with the Holy Spirit and (I imagine) joyfully shouting, "Look . . . I see heaven open and the Son of Man standing at the right hand of God[!]"[3] The kind of suffering God calls us into will always lead to joy and satisfaction in him. So, for example, since wisdom teaches that marrying a Nabal will not lead to joy, then we

2. e.g., Matthew 5:12; Acts 5:41; Romans 5:3–5; Hebrews 10:34; James 1:2–4; 1 Peter 4:13

3. Acts 7:56

can know that God will never command us to marry a Nabal. God will never require obedience that is truly bad for us.

This leads me to the second point. God is the same yesterday, today, and forever.[4] He does not change his mind, and he does not contradict his word.[5] He will not ask you to do something now that he has blatantly told you not to do in his word. If he has said it is bad to be yoked to an unbeliever, he won't change his mind in your case. If he has outlined principles of wisdom for dating in his word, he will not tell you to ignore them all when it comes time to actually choose a spouse.

The third point is in response to an objection people may have to the first two points. If you are familiar with the Bible, what seems like an exception to what I'm saying in terms of marriage may come to mind: the story of Hosea and Gomer. In the book of Hosea, we read God's command that Hosea should "marry a promiscuous woman and have children with her."[6] God is specifically commanding a man to do the exact opposite of everything I am proposing. Does this mean that God might call someone to do the same today?

We must be careful when using stories from biblical history, especially from the lives of the prophets, as proof texts. In Scripture, God does ask people, primarily prophets, to do things that would be unwise or maybe even sinful in any other circumstance. Think about God telling Abraham to sacrifice his son, Isaac, in Genesis 22. Is this proof that God wants people to kill their children, and that they should trust that he will remedy it in some way? Of course not! At one point, God commands Isaiah to walk out in public wearing no clothes at all![7] Is this proof that God wills his children to be nudists? Of course not! In Ezekiel 4:4–17, God commands Ezekiel to lie on his side for over a year, cooking his food over a fire fueled by dung. (Don't worry, God lets him use

4. Exodus 3:14; Malachi 3:6; James 1:17; see Hebrews 13:8
5. See, e.g., Numbers 23:19; Psalm 119:160; Hebrews 6:18
6. Hosea 1:2
7. Isaiah 20:2

cow dung instead of the original plan of human dung.) Is this an indication of how we should be eating dinner tomorrow night?

You see my point. In all these instances, God is commanding an action as a one-time sign for the historical people of Israel. These commands are not reinforced or repeated in any other passage of Scripture. We should not read the stories of Abraham, Isaiah, Ezekiel, or Hosea as one-for-one instruction for our lives. Our reflex interpretation of a perceived voice telling us to marry someone that Scripture says we shouldn't ought to match our interpretation of a voice telling us to kill our child, walk around naked, or cook our food with poop—not God's.

I understand that this may be a sensitive topic for some. Believe me, I really do understand. Whenever someone insinuated that maybe I wouldn't or shouldn't marry my former fiancée, I completely ignored them. "*God told me to*" rang through my head again and again and again. The truth is, he didn't; it might have been me, or it might have been a demon, but it wasn't God. God would not tell me to do something that contradicted the wisdom in his word. And he will not for you either. God's will for your marriage is that you would be joyfully married to someone who isn't perfect but is both compatible with you and full of character: loving, godly, and desiring to be righteous in all things. He loves to give good gifts to his children and does not desire that you should be stuck in a relationship that falls short of his best.

One last note, for those who are already married. If you are currently married to someone whose character is less than what is outlined in the last two chapters, remember that God is still good. I believe his ideal for marriage is not the one you are experiencing. I believe he wants strong, mutually sanctifying marriages for all his children. But that does not mean your marriage is hopeless. He has a perfect plan for your life, even now, and he promises to use all things for your good if you love and obey him.[8] Scripture repeatedly encourages spouses to stay committed and hopeful, even if they are married to an unbeliever. Who knows how God may use you to influence, sanctify, or even save your spouse if you are

8. Romans 8:28

faithful?[9] Never forget, "Let us not become weary in doing good, for at the proper time we will reap a harvest if we do not give up."[10] Don't give up; we have a God who turns ashes into beauty.[11]

REFLECTION QUESTIONS

1. What advantages can you think of to dating within your home church? What might be the benefits of dating someone as a friend, instead of more intimately, in this context?
2. What do you think of the other exhortations in this chapter? How can you apply these truths in your own life or use them to encourage someone you know, in a dating context and beyond?

9. 1 Corinthians 7:16; 1 Peter 3:1–2
10. Galatians 6:9
11. See Isaiah 61:3

12

You Don't Know Unless You Ask (Others)

Dating with the purpose of intentionally discovering compatibility and character is both way easier and way harder than the average relationship. It is much easier because it is much less messy. It is straightforward and focused. It is more difficult because determining someone's character is a daunting task! How good is good enough? What about their weaknesses? How much imperfection is acceptable? How can I be sure they really have those good qualities?

No one is meant to figure these questions out alone, and it is essential that you do not try to. As we will see shortly, it is wisest to involve others in your relationship as much as possible. The question is not only what *you* see in the other person, but what *others* see in them and what *others* think of the two of you together.

The first person you need to ask to give insight into your relationship is God. Pray. A lot. Pray before you enter a relationship. Pray throughout the relationship. Pray as you consider marriage. Pray continually.[1] If you persistently pray for wisdom and

1. 1 Thessalonians 5:17

for God's guidance in your relationship, he *promises* to give it to you.[2] And certainly invite others to pray for you as well.

Although we do not get much of a glimpse into the prayer lives of Ruth and Boaz (it is hard to imagine that they weren't strong), we do get indications that prayer was involved in their relationship. Admittedly, it is not prayer in the way we think of prayer, but blessing someone in the name of the Lord seems clearly to have the same heart behind it as praying for them. Naomi blesses the future relationships of her daughters-in-law at the story's start,[3] Boaz blesses Ruth,[4] Naomi blesses Boaz,[5] and the community blesses both Ruth and Boaz as they begin their marriage.[6] Prayer surrounds the relationship from beginning to end.

It is imperative to not only involve God in relationship decisions but to rely on him completely for guidance. He is the all-knowing, all-powerful God. Of course, much of that guidance he has already given in the Bible; follow it. Beyond that, I personally find myself praying that he would communicate using the "Closed Door Test." "God, if this relationship is a bad idea, please make it painfully obvious. Close the door on the relationship. Don't let it even start. I do not want to marry someone outside of your will." If you continue asking, seeking, and knocking in this way, you can be sure he will answer.[7]

God will guide you directly, but he will also guide you through others in your life. It is in this way that we see him guide Ruth and Boaz. In the second chapter of Ruth, Ruth spends a long, sweat-filled day observing Boaz's character. By all accounts, he seems like a *good man, full of character*. But what reassurance to know that Naomi agrees! "He has not stopped showing his kindness to the living and the dead," she says in verse 20. (This refers to Boaz honoring Elimelek and Mahlon by caring for their widows.) From this,

2. See Luke 11:9; James 1:5
3. Ruth 1:9
4. Ruth 2:12
5. Ruth 2:20
6. Ruth 4:11–12
7. Luke 11:9

Ruth learns that not only does Naomi agree that Boaz *is* righteous, but she learns that he has been this way for a long time—he has *not stopped* showing his kindness. His character was not an act for Ruth's sake. His character is established and evident whether Ruth is around or not.

We also see, in verse 22, that Ruth has a trustworthy relational advisor in Naomi: "It will be good for you, my daughter, to go with the women who work for [Boaz]." Of course, Ruth's safety and the two women's food supply are the primary concerns, but in Naomi's words we can tell she *approves* of Ruth continuing to spend time with Boaz. Ruth clearly respects and trusts Naomi—she is, after all, the reason Ruth started following the Lord. Her insight into Boaz's character and her recommendation give Ruth confidence in moving forward. The importance of this insight and counsel only escalates in chapter 3. In verses 1–5, Naomi advises Ruth that it's time she got married to Boaz! (Again, we'll discuss the righteousness of her plan in chapter 14.) It is only at this point that Ruth moves forward in pursuit of marriage.

Just as Ruth was greatly influenced by others' view of Boaz, Boaz is greatly influenced by others' view of Ruth. We have already discussed Boaz's reliance on others in discovering who "the new girl" was, but we see his continued reliance as the story progresses. In Ruth 2:11–12, we see that the foundation for Boaz being impressed by Ruth was *others'* reports about her: "*I've been told* all about what you have done for your mother-in-law. May the Lord repay you for what you have done. May you be richly rewarded by the Lord" (emphasis mine). Based on how favorable Boaz's reaction to the reports was, along with the general flow of the book, we can safely infer that not only Boaz, but everybody was impressed by Ruth's character. This evaluation is confirmed in 3:11: "All the people of my town know that you are a woman of noble character."

There are a couple levels of cool at work in the previous verse. First, it just bears repeating, Ruth is a Proverbs 31 woman of noble character in the eyes of the townspeople. That's just the coolest thing ever. The second applies to all the verses we've just read: there's got to be a reason he knows what the townspeople are saying. Has he been specifically asking them, or has everyone talked about it of their own accord? Either way, as with Ruth and Naomi, Boaz really *knows* Ruth is awesome because *others* have confirmed it. I wonder how many townspeople added something along the lines of, "Don't mess this up, Boaz."

Neither Ruth nor Boaz relied only on their personal assessment; they both got input from others. It is important to notice that the input came from people who knew *both* of them. Naomi knew Boaz, but she also knew Ruth extremely well. This made her a great person to give input on Boaz's character, but also on the relationship as a whole. She could answer both whether Boaz was a good man *and* whether he was a good match for Ruth. Similarly, the townspeople *knew* Boaz. They were familiar with him. Demographic studies suggest that villages at this time ordinarily had only a few hundred people. The population might have been even smaller because the famine caused some inhabitants to die or emigrate.[8] In other words, this was a tight-knit community. The people there could tell Boaz with comfort and confidence that Ruth was a Proverbs 31 woman because, as with Naomi, they knew them both well.

Relationships, even godly, character-focused ones, are emotional. When you are fond of someone, it can be hard to see and think clearly about their character. And even when you do see clearly, you cannot know how that person acts when you're not around. For all these reasons, it is *imperative* that you rely on wise, godly people in your life to help you determine the character of the person you are dating. Proverbs 11:14: "Where there is no guidance, a people falls, but in an abundance of counselors there is safety" (ESV). God wants us to have counsel in our lives—how much more critical for a decision that will have lifelong and perhaps eternal repercussions!

As with Ruth's example, it makes most sense to involve your families as a first priority. If you are younger, you really ought to talk to your own parents *and* the other person's parents about a possible relationship. They know and are responsible for the

8. Keener and Walton, NKJV Cultural Backgrounds Study Bible, 473.

person you are interested in. Establishing this rapport early and continuing it throughout the relationship will go a long way, especially if the time for engagement comes. If you are older, though their parents are not responsible for them in the same way, this is probably still a wise step. Of course, if either set of parents is unsaved, wisdom and other counsel will be required, but involving parents is a very wise move.

Aside from parents, your local church—your pastors and spiritual mentors in particular—is an invaluable source of wisdom and prayer to invite into your relationship early and often. In today's age, many underestimate the gift God has designed us to receive through the church. It is a wise person who recognizes God's design and takes advantage of the opportunity to spend time with the person they are dating in the context of their church. To have so many wise and godly people give input and advice for your relationship is a true gift. To have pastors truly shepherding you in this way is irreplaceable.

Lean most on the wise and trusted people in your life, but ask everyone you can about your potential spouse-to-be—whether they've known them their whole life or they've talked to them for five minutes.

This process can be a little scary. *What if they don't like him? What if she's not good enough for them? What if they make a bad impression?* The good news is these aren't really concerns when you find a winner winner chicken dinner: their true character will shine through before too long. When I was courting Kylie, I absolutely loved asking others about her. We had been together for a few weeks when Kylie first came with me to my parents' place to meet them and six of my siblings (talk about pressure!). Afterward, I asked my parents and other family members to individually tell me three words to describe her. She spent a lot of time with my siblings one-on-one in the few hours she was there, so there were several chances for her true colors to shine through. The consensus was that Kylie was *godly, pure, and winsome*. I'll take that.

My family knows me very well, but they only knew her briefly at that point. So I also asked trustworthy people who had known

Kylie for years. They had nothing but good things to say. I asked my spiritual mentors. Huge fans. I also relied on my roommates, who spent a lot of time with both of us. All green lights. Like I said, I talked to everyone I could. My favorite experience was when I asked my roommate's sister-in-law, whom I trusted both because my roommate spoke so highly of her and because she was very clearly a wise and devoted Christian; I knew she would shoot it straight with me. She talked to Kylie for ten minutes and told me, "Don't ever let her go."

The person you're dating may fool you, but they're not going to fool everybody. As you seek to gain a clear understanding of your person of interest's character, do yourself a favor and confirm or deny what you see with a hundred other testimonies. Ask those who know you both to any degree for an honest evaluation of that person and of the relationship. Find out who they are when you aren't around. Find out what kind of person they were before they met you.

By the way, did you notice that Ruth, and especially Boaz, did not wait until they were already in a "relationship" to do this character-investigating and counsel-seeking? You don't have to either. In my experience, it is wisest to do as much investigating and counsel-seeking *before* you start dating someone. At the point when you like everything you see and everything you've heard from others, but you need a closer look, *then* seek to enter into a dating relationship. You might even start by having a couple intentional conversations before you actually enter the relationship. This process eliminates a lot of unnecessary boyfriends, girlfriends, and baggage.

If you want to reap the rewards of dating with others' input, the point should be made that this means you *have to* spend time around others as a couple. If you want to reap the *most* rewards, do this as often as possible. I get it: spending time "just the two of you" is fun. Sometimes, one-on-one time is even necessary to discuss more private matters (like where you two see the relationship going). But if you want to marry someone with strong character, it is best to *know* they have strong character rather than being *pretty sure*. Others will confirm or deny what you see in the person you are dating.

Spending time with others will also allow you to see how the person you are dating treats other people and how they act in a group. Practically speaking, spending a lot of time with others, up close and frequently, has no substitute when it comes to making sure of their character. How valuable is the parent, the pastor, and the godly, honest mutual friend whom you let see a quality picture of your potential marriage to come—how much more valuable when there are several. In conjunction with much prayer, these kinds of people will ensure you enter a good and godly marriage. If that is your desire, don't date alone.

REFLECTION QUESTIONS

1. Do you discuss your dating interests with your parents? Would anything in your relationship with them need to change for these conversations to be most successful?
2. How well do you know your pastor(s)? What would it look like to establish a relationship with them that would make seeking their dating counsel seem natural?
3. Do you know other people in your church whom you would trust to give you good counsel in a relationship? If not, what wise Christians do you know that could fill this need?
4. What are the benefits of not dating alone, according to this chapter and otherwise?

13

When You Know, You Know

Relationships should be founded upon mutual interest, attraction, compatibility, and, most importantly, character, as evaluated by those involved in the relationship and those who bear witness to it. If a person does not pass the tests to a proper degree, they are not the person you should marry. In this last chapter of this part of the book, we will discuss how to complete a dating relationship.

The first point of this chapter is this: if you know the person you are dating is not the person you will marry, you should break up with them as soon as possible. Breaking up is hard. It is not at all fun. But let's be frank: delaying an inevitable breakup is a waste of your time and theirs and only makes things worse. If you are in that scenario, you need to do the hard thing and end the relationship.

The good news is that this is so much easier to do if you have dated wisely up to that point. If you have followed the advice of this book thus far, then the only statement you've made in deciding to date someone is, "I want to see if you are the person I want to marry." All breaking up says, in this case, is, "I do not wish to *marry* you." It is not a rejection of them as a person; it is a rejection of them as a spouse. What a world of difference! There ought not to be as much hurt involved in this as there is in a "normal" breakup. There are high stakes and high standards involved in the decision. *Most* people are not the kind of person you'll want to marry. We shouldn't be offended or heartbroken when we aren't that person for someone else. And you definitely don't want to be married to someone who *doesn't* think you're marriage material.

Still, breakups can be delicate, and it takes some tact and wisdom to know how to navigate one well, on either end. We will deal with those specifics in chapter 19. For now, remember, when you know you want to break up with someone, don't put it off.

Of course, sometimes you "know" in the *other* way. You know, "I want to marry this person! They aren't perfect, they sin, they've got flaws, and I'm going to discover many more, but we are headed the same direction at the same speed, we both love Jesus, and, by golly, I think they're spectacular." So, what next? You decide it's time . . . to wait four years so you can make some money. Or perhaps go do something you always wanted to do before you're "tied down" for good. Or you decide, "Well, there's no reason to rush! Let's date a few more years, just in case." Even if someone rejected this thinking when entering a relationship and intended on dating for marriage, it is not uncommon for the prospect of an *actual* marriage to give people cold feet.

Is there something wrong with holding off on marriage in this way? Again, I cannot say this as a blanket statement for all people in all situations, but the general issue with waiting is that it stands in total contradiction to the wisdom of God's word. We have already talked about the repeated refrain from the Song of Solomon of not awakening love prematurely. But also consider Paul's advice to single people in 1 Corinthians: to paraphrase, stay single if at all possible, or else get on with it and get married![1] Boaz and Ruth certainly agreed with this sentiment. When Ruth knew that she wanted to marry Boaz, she approached him, almost literally, immediately afterward.[2] When Boaz registered what was going on, he quickly made up his mind (can you tell he'd put some

1. 1 Corinthians 7:8–9
2. Ruth 3:5–6

thought into it before that point?) and told her they could, Lord willing, be married *the next day*.[3]

What was the rush? It seems to me that there was *no* rush, just excitement. They knew they wanted to be married, so they got married. That's all there was to it! To put it in the terms of the Song of Solomon, love had awoken, and it was time. Consider the alternative put forth by Paul in 1 Corinthians 7: burning with passion—having the desire to be together and intimate in every way but delaying that reality. That kind of approach wouldn't benefit Boaz and Ruth in any way. They would be tied down to each other, in a sense, and held back from surrendering unhindered to God's will—not in the healthy context of marriage but in the limbo of "we're kind of engaged, but not really."

Just as there was no sense for Boaz and Ruth to wait, there is no sense for us to. When you know, you know. And once you know, there's no reason to wait. Men, step into your role as her leader, ask her father for her hand, and put a ring on it. Waiting brings no worthwhile benefits. Waiting shows that you are committed to someone but not fully. Waiting forces you both into the strange situation, to borrow from an earlier analogy, of having both little time *and* no money; you are refusing to experience the full blessedness of singleness or of marriage. It is a place you are not meant to remain overly long.

People justify waiting for all sorts of reasons: they are not ready to have children, they are not financially ready to support a family, they want to finish school first—you name it. These may be valid reasons to wait to get married, but, as we discussed earlier in the book, if you are not ready to get married, then you probably shouldn't date to begin with. This is not to be legalistic. I cannot call being in a long-term relationship in "status limbo" a sin, but it does seem to go against God's will for your relationship (awakened love, burning with passion, unfree to serve the Lord unhindered, etc.).

God's will is that dating ends in marriage or singleness. In delaying marriage, you are committing yourself to less than God's best, and I do not think you can expect God's best results from

3. Ruth 3:13

delaying his desires. Certainly, there is a difference between delaying a marriage until you are more financially stable and delaying a marriage to achieve all your hopes and dreams. But perhaps, in either case, you have become guilty of awakening love before its time. A person who is convinced they should accomplish certain goals before marriage should probably wait until those goals are accomplished before they begin dating. As I said in chapter 3, this requires a great trust in God, but it is for the best.

In ancient biblical times, there seems to have been a similar understanding. Though there is no consensus among scholars on the specific amount of time, the average period of betrothal seems to have been about a year. Remember, "dating" did not exist, as such, so this year would have served primarily to allow the husband- and wife-to-be to get to know each other and to allow time for the character of those involved to be checked and proved (in addition to giving the families time to plan the wedding).[4] A year was considered an adequate amount of time to *know* it was a good match, and when they knew, they were married. In other words, when they knew, they knew! If you have entered into a relationship wisely, understanding that marriage may be near when you start it, then you, too, should abide by the practice of "When you know, you know." As soon as you are *convinced* of their character, that's it. That is the goal of dating: to make sure they are a good three-legged race partner and to make sure they will bring you closer to God. Once that's locked in, here is Paul's, Boaz's, Jewish tradition's, and my own encouragement to you: put a ring on it and get married!

If you are a little apprehensive, maybe hearing a bit more of our story will help. Kylie and I got married five months after we started courting; we were engaged for five weeks of those five months; and, for two of those months, I was in India, and we were not allowed to communicate. You might say we really "dated" for a whopping *eight weeks*! But we knew. How did we know? Because we had studied each other's character. Because we had talked to many, many people who had also studied our characters. Because

4. Jones, "Divorce and Remarriage," 74–75.

we had gotten relationship insight and advice from many counselors in our lives. And, for me, because while I was in India, I asked God to show me all over again that I should marry Kylie. I had thought I wanted to marry her before I left, and if he could show me again, just as clearly, once I was home, then that would be all the confirmation I needed. We got engaged less than a month and a half after I returned.

I remember my proposal very clearly: we were hanging out one night (I was working on an online quiz due at midnight, and she was keeping me company), and something overcame me. I had ordered her engagement ring—it would be ready the next day—but I didn't want to wait until then. I wanted to be engaged *that night*. I couldn't shake the desire. After I finished my quiz, I turned to Kylie and said, "Kylie . . . I need to go pray." So, I got up, went to her kitchen for about ten minutes, and tried to ask God if this was right. I mean, what was I even going to propose with? I knew I wanted to marry her—that had been settled—but was *now* really the best time? I hadn't planned exactly how I wanted to propose, but I knew it wasn't going to be *this*. I rummaged through the drawers, asking God what I could put on her finger . . . and I saw this old, beat-up green twist tie. "*Ha!*" I told myself, "*I don't think so*." I continued to search and search and found *nothing*. I looked again at the twist tie, laughed to myself, and said, "*God, are you sure?*" Committing to it in my heart, I wrapped the twist tie around my pinky to fit Kylie's slender finger, put it in my pocket, and walked back into the living room. I sat down, looked at Kylie, and said, with all my heart, "Kylie . . . I need to go pray again."

Give me a break; it seemed like the stupidest idea ever! I took five more minutes to really try to think and pray it through, and I decided that this was the way I really wanted to do it. I went into the room, looked Kylie in the eye, told her I loved her (for the first time), and asked her to marry me. She said yes. She wore her totally fake ring proudly the next day until I picked up the real one and re-proposed in front of our friends the next night. She really loved how it all happened (guys, you gotta know your girl). We still have and treasure that green twist tie ring.

My point in sharing all of this is that we didn't wait for everything to be "perfect." The whole time we were courting, we were flat broke. Kylie had five part-time jobs, and I had one. I was still in school, studying to be an elementary school teacher. I had student loans we would have to pay off, and Kylie had debt from the car she had just bought (the financial prospects were *excellent*). She stopped working shortly after we got married because of the severity of her morning sickness in pregnancy; our cumulative earnings for our first year of marriage were about $6,000. Would it have been wise to wait until we had a little more financial stability? I really don't think so. God provided! Matthew 6:33: "But seek first [God's] kingdom and his righteousness, and all these things *will be given to you as well*" (emphasis mine). Kylie and I have made seeking God's kingdom the highest priority in our lives. We have done that very, very imperfectly, and we have made plenty of mistakes along the way (wouldn't recommend going into debt for a car, for instance), but God has yet to fail to provide for our financial needs. Not once have we felt poor; not once have we wished we had waited.

Because we decided to get married "immediately," as Boaz and Ruth did, we have our beautiful daughter. We have three beautiful sons. We have a story of God's providence that we absolutely would not have otherwise. And God has sanctified us greatly through it all. I am not suggesting that our timeline is the ideal timeline, and no, it is not a sin to wait to be married for financial reasons. But I do think it is a missed opportunity. Waiting is missing out on an adventure God wants you to have. It is missing out on an opportunity to go through a growth season as *one flesh* instead of *two*. (Not to mention it is the *way less fun* version of making some money or finishing a degree, if either is the reason you're deciding to wait.)

One final encouragement for those who can't decide if they really *do* know or not. What if this one isn't "the one"? And my encouragement to you is that, biblically, "the one" does not seem to exist. The idea of a "soulmate" who is out there somewhere just waiting to complete you is one that our culture finds utterly romantic.

However, it is an idea that comes from pagan philosophy, and certainly *not* the Bible. According to the Bible, the *only* "one" out there that will complete you is the Lord Jesus Christ. *He* is the one that you were made for, the one that will make you whole.

Of course, that might not be the kind of "one" you have in mind. Perhaps you are thinking more about the person that God wants you to marry—a particular individual that God, being infinitely wise, knows would be your ideal mate. Truly, though, what a stressful thought! For simplicity's sake, let's just say that a quarter of the world's almost 1 billion men/women your age are eligible. That's literally a 0.0004 percent chance of "getting it right." To put it mildly, the odds are not quite in your favor. Buying into the idea of "the one," regardless of who you marry, opens the door to being forever plagued by the thought, "*What if my spouse isn't the one? What if I should have married someone else?*"

Not that any of that is proof, but it certainly makes me *hope* that there's not just one person we are intended to marry. For concrete proof, consider this: when we think about God's instructions for our lives, it is apparent that he generally wants us to live by principles and not time-and-place-specific commands. We do not (and should not) stop to ask God, "Should I read my Bible this morning?" or, "Should I be kind today?" or, "Should I be a hard worker this week?" The reason we do not need to ask these questions is that God has already told us the answer in his word. He has said these things are good, and he wants us to use wisdom to do them at any time of day and in any location that he provides.

Think about the story of the Good Samaritan.[5] When the Samaritan comes across the man who is stripped, beaten, and half dead, he does not pause to say, "Gee, I'm gonna have to pray about this one." God put the man in his path, and he wisely decides to love this stranger who desperately needs his help.

The Bible seems to indicate that the same way of thinking applies to romantic relationships. We need not delay marrying a godly person in fear that they are not "the one" when God has already told us the type of person we should marry. I say this with

5. Luke 10:25–37

confidence because of the wording of two passages of Scripture. First, in Numbers 36, when there is concern regarding what will happen to the inheritance of the clan of Gilead if Zelophehad's daughters marry outside the clan (you'll have to read the passage in more detail if you want to really get it), the LORD commands, "They may marry *anyone they please* as long as they marry within their father's tribal clan"[6] (emphasis mine). Similarly, in 1 Corinthians 7:39: "A woman is bound to her husband as long as he lives. But if her husband dies, she is *free to marry anyone she wishes*, but he must belong to the Lord" (emphasis mine). According to both of these passages, a woman is to marry a *type* of man (one "within their father's tribal clan" or one who "belongs to the Lord"), not a *particular* man. The language is *not* "she is free to marry the one God chooses for her." This means that in searching for a spouse, like in other decisions, we can expect to live by principles and not time-and-place-specific commands. We are to trust the wisdom of God's word in looking for a spouse, but we need not wait for God's go-ahead in neon lights when we find a godly person that we and others agree is a good fit, and one that God does not "close the door" on. Assuming they meet the character requirements ("but he must belong to the Lord"), we are *free to marry anyone we wish*.

How freeing! How wonderful! *Could* I have married someone besides Kylie? Yes! Does that mean she is not "the one"? Not at all. I married Kylie because she is godly and because I *wanted* to spend the rest of my life with her. And that is *exactly* the type of woman that God wanted me to marry. I was looking for *a* "one," not *the* "one." God's wisdom and biblical principles led me to her, not a spiritual treasure map (i.e., signs and wonders).

I realize I say all of this as the husband of Kylie, a woman that was led by God to marry a bearded soccer player who led worship, had a big family, liked math, etc., a year to the day after she wrote him a letter. And it strikes me as funny that, while looking for a wife for Isaac, Abraham's servant literally says, "May it be that when I say to a young woman, 'Please let down your jar that I may have a drink,' and she says, 'Drink, and I'll water your camels

6. v. 6

too'—let her be *the one* you have chosen for your servant Isaac" (emphasis mine).[7] And my response to both of these is that God *can* lead us to a particular person, but we should not *expect* him to.

Imagine being Abraham's servant. You are in a foreign land where you know nobody, and you are looking for the perfect match for your master's son. I can understand the man wanting a little help. The fact that God graciously gives it to him does not mean that it is the biblical norm.

As for Kylie, I couldn't say why God thought it was a good idea to lead her pretty obviously to me. It's definitely a super cool story though. And talk about confirmation. Perhaps he knew that she'd need the reassurance, or maybe he just knew it'd be a really good evangelism tool—we'll forever get to say, "Our living and active God did *that*."

All of this to say that if you apply the wisdom of God's word—searching for the kind of man or woman that he says will make a good spouse, getting input from godly advisors, and praying for his guidance and wisdom in the process—*that* is how you can expect him to lead you into a wonderful marriage to the man or woman beyond your wildest dreams. It is possible he will guide you in more "supernatural" ways, but it is more likely that he will not.

So, are you ready? Have you done your research? Is the person you are dating the person you want to spend the rest of your life with? Do your homework, ask God and those around you, and when you know, you'll know.

REFLECTION QUESTIONS

1. What things do you want to have done before getting married?
2. Do you agree that it is unwise to delay marriage when you know you want to marry someone? If not, what exceptions would you make to this principle?

7. Genesis 24:14

3. Do you believe that God will provide for your needs if you are seeking to do his will? What, if anything, makes it difficult to trust him to the degree described in this chapter?
4. What are your reactions to the claim that "the one" doesn't exist? What would be the effects of believing either way on this issue?

PART FOUR

Avoiding Brokenness

14

Acting Unmarried

AT THIS POINT IN the book, we have worked through a biblical foundation for dating, the importance of singleness, and how to find a godly spouse. We will now turn our attention to avoiding brokenness. I am completely guessing here, but I'd say that about one out of three movies, one out of two Shakespeare plays, and ninety-five out of ninety-six Taylor Swift songs are about heartbreak in some way. When it comes to modern relationships, heartbreak is the norm. And though we love the plays, movies, and songs, we do *not* love heartbreak. This raises the question: Is it possible to avoid it?

By now, you've seen that the kind of dating described in this book is very different from what is typical. The definition is different, the focus is different, and, as we're about to see, the parameters are different. This is why some people decide to call this kind of "dating" a different name entirely. When Kylie and I dated, we called ourselves "courtship partners." We didn't come up with the name, but we liked it because we thought of it as a witnessing tool. It instigated questions like, "You guys are *what*?" It led to opportunities to talk about why we dated the way we dated.

It is in these chapters that a "courting" mentality shows itself as definitely distinct from a "dating" one. For clarity's sake, from here on out, I will refer to worldly, unhealthy dating as "dating," and biblical, healthy dating as "courting." Generally, courting is considered to be distinguished from dating by its "formal" and "rigid" protocols: A gentleman in a top hat asks the parents for permission to "call on" their daughter. With their consent, the gentleman then goes on long walks with their daughter while the family follows about twenty feet behind. If all goes well, he'll pay the bride price for her. We hear "courting" as a society and consider it an antique form of dating—back when marriages were still arranged and people weren't free to enjoy life. And so we reject the whole notion of courting and attempt to date without inhibition. Boyfriends and girlfriends fall in love, share their lives, and often have sex, all without committing to a covenant for life. And it *doesn't work*. It leads to unhealthy relationships, broken families, fatherless homes, ailing societies, and children who will likely start the cycle all over again—sometimes at an even younger age and with even worse consequences (having sex at an early age is associated with higher rates of risky sexual behaviors, drug use, and incarceration[1]).

What is the answer then? How do we engage in relationships that won't leave us broken without feeling arbitrarily tied down to a set of ancient rules and practices? The answer is biblical courting.

Biblical courting can be defined as a relationship in which the man and woman involved (hopefully you've seen that courting isn't for those who are still acting like children) seriously consider marriage while behaving like what they actually are: unmarried. That's right, we're back to the original hypothesis of this book: "Biblically, a boyfriend or a girlfriend is supposed to be a type of *friend*." There have been hints at the wisdom of this definition before now, but in these coming chapters, I hope to make you fully convinced. Let's begin by, again, examining our favorite Old Testament couple.

Boaz and Ruth each conducted themselves according to a courtship model, but it is easier to see in Boaz's actions. Consider

1. STD Surveillance Network, "SSuN Special Focus Report."

all of Boaz's actions toward Ruth: he let her collect barley from his field,[2] he instructed his men not to touch her and allowed her to drink his water,[3] he shared his food with her at mealtime,[4] he instructed his men to make her gleaning easier by doing some of the work for her,[5] he invited her to come back for the rest of the harvest,[6] he gave her a gift of six measures of barley,[7] and *then* he married her. In all of these actions, Boaz *never* crossed the line from acting "unmarried" to acting "married." Not once. Remember the job of a husband: to lead and care for his wife. Boaz did not act this way toward Ruth. He did not collect the barley for Ruth. He did not say, "You sit back and let me take care of you, baby." He did not thresh the barley for her. He did not take it back to town for her or have his men do so. He was kind, he was respectful, he went beyond the requirements of the law for her,[8] he was even a little protective of her, but he never acted like Ruth's husband before he actually was. He only ever acted as a type of friend. Affectionate? Definitely. Intimate? Never.

Though it is hard to see as clearly, Ruth acts the same way toward Boaz. Her actions are completely devoid of promiscuity and wifely devotion to Boaz. The would-be exception is clearly Ruth's midnight escapade to . . . uncover Boaz's feet? What is that about? At last, we will discuss exactly that.

Biblical commentators interpret this scene in many different ways, ranging from completely innocent to overtly sexual, with just about everything in between claimed by one commentator or another. So, what's the truth?

Ruth 3:1–15 describes this scene, which we will analyze one step at a time. Step one: Ruth washes up, puts on perfume, and changes into her best clothes. Is this meant to be provocative? A

2. Ruth 2:8
3. Ruth 2:9
4. Ruth 2:14
5. Ruth 2:15–16
6. Ruth 2:21
7. Ruth 3:15
8. See, e.g., Leviticus 19:9–10

way to entice Boaz by flaunting her body? If we are letting Scripture interpret Scripture, the answer seems to be no. Interestingly, we read about David doing almost the *exact* same thing in 2 Samuel 12:19–20. After David had fasted and spent every night on the ground dressed in sackcloth, pleading with God to spare the life of his son, we are told:

> David noticed that his attendants were whispering among themselves, and he realized the child was dead. "Is the child dead?" he asked. "Yes," they replied, "he is dead." Then David got up from the ground. After he had washed, put on lotions and changed his clothes, he went into the house of the Lord and worshiped. Then he went to his own house, and at his request they served him food, and he ate.

It seems, then, this is *not* a provocative action; in both cases, the message communicated by these actions is, "I'm done mourning, now." David had been fasting and mourning for his dying son, and Ruth's husband had died not long prior to meeting Boaz. By washing and purtying up, Ruth is simply sending a clear message to Boaz: "I'm available."[9]

The next part of the scene seems kind of strange: Ruth waits until Boaz is sleeping, then uncovers his feet and lies down by him until he wakes up. Some people see in this a sexual action of some sort. In truth, there is nothing to suggest that this is sexual. A straightforward reading of the text indicates that Ruth uncovered Boaz's actual feet so that he would wake up after a time.[10] A personal hypothesis about the motivation for this has to do with discretion. What if Ruth went out in broad daylight this way to talk to Boaz about marriage, and he turned her down? Everyone would know. I believe Naomi and Ruth both wanted this encounter to be private. Still, the approach might be a little startling, so care would need to be taken to make sure Boaz received it well—hence planning the visit for when Boaz was in good spirits and allowing

9. ESV Study Bible, 481.

10. Ruth 3:7

him to wake up more "naturally" than if he were shaken awake, for example.

A deeper reading of the text reveals more (still honorable) significance. Again, looking to the life of David, we see a similar type of action spoken of by Abigail just before she marries the king. In 1 Samuel 25:41, after David's servants have approached Abigail about becoming David's wife, Abigail bows her face to the ground and says, "I am your servant and am ready to serve you and wash the feet of my lord's servants." This verse is literally surrounded only by verses that speak about her marrying David. The interpretation of her words is clear, then: Abigail accepts the offer! She declares that she is willing to *submit* (i.e., be a "servant") to David as his wife. Through Ruth's actions, we see the same exact heart. By uncovering Boaz's feet, she wakes him up. By lying at his feet, she communicates, "I am willing to 'be your servant' and submit to you as your wife."

After saying this, Ruth adds something else that might seem questionable: "Spread the corner of your garment over me."[11] But again, this is in no way Ruth "getting into bed" with Boaz. "Corner of a garment" can also be translated as "wings." If this translation is taken, Ruth is asking Boaz to spread his wings over her—like he indicates God does in Ruth 2:12—so that she can take refuge under him as her husband.[12] Even if "corner of a garment" *doesn't* mean "wings," but the actual corner of his garment, then we still know what Ruth meant by Boaz's reaction: "If possible, I *will* do this."[13] Ruth is not proposing a current action but a future one: marriage. I am convinced that in all her actions and words—washing, putting on perfume, dressing up, visiting Boaz by night, uncovering his feet, lying by his feet, and asking him to spread his garment (or wings) over her—Ruth is honorably suggesting they get married while *not acting like she is Boaz's wife.*

In the beginning of the book, I discussed that there are only three categories for relationships according to the Bible and that

11. Ruth 3:9

12. ESV Study Bible, 480.

13. See Ruth 3:10–13

"dating" falls into the category of friendship. In the case of Boaz and Ruth, we see that this definition was true. Aside from Ruth's suggestion that they get married, *everything* Boaz and Ruth did in their relationship very comfortably falls under the category of "friendly." Boaz certainly seemed to take special notice of Ruth, but all of his actions toward her were *unmarried* actions. In other words, it is conceivable that Boaz would do any one of those things for *any other woman*: feed them, serve them, and give them generous gifts. Similarly, Ruth, not counting her final actions toward him, could have conceivably treated *any other man* the way she treated Boaz throughout the story. The only difference was the way they felt about each other.

In a courting relationship, partners will undoubtedly develop feelings for each other. They will become more affectionate than "just friends" as the relationship continues. But, like Boaz and Ruth, it is essential that they don't act intimately until they're married. Why? For now, let us say because God's shining example of a courtship did not and because experience has taught many, like myself, again and again that doing otherwise is never truly beneficial. As we continue, we will see that even stronger reasons can be added to this answer.

REFLECTION QUESTIONS

1. This chapter again asserts that a courting relationship is meant to be a type of friendship. Has your response to this claim changed since the beginning of the book?
2. What do you think about the example of Boaz and Ruth at this point in the book? Is there anything about their relationship that you particularly appreciate?

15

Physical Unmarriage

MARRIAGE IS THE UNION of two souls. When God says, "The two shall become one," he means more than just sexual union. Marriage binds two souls physically, but also emotionally, and even spiritually. This is why a husband is called to provide for his wife's physical *and* emotional *and* spiritual needs. Because he and she are one, her needs are intertwined with his own needs, and loving her in all these ways is the same thing as loving himself.[1] This beautiful, mysterious union is meant to take place between two married people or not at all. Again, Scripture only ever describes marriage as the proper context for "becoming one flesh," and we know this is not a process to be experienced more than once, if we can help it: "What God has joined together, let no one separate."[2]

Two unmarried people are not meant to act married. This does not mean you cannot have feelings for your courtship partner. It means you should not do anything that will in any way make you "one" with your courtship partner, physically, emotionally, or spiritually.

1. Ephesians 5:28–29
2. Mark 10:9

Let's unpack these one at a time, starting with physical boundaries. The first time Kylie and I held hands was in a moment during a walk together before we were courting. We were talking about entering a relationship and decided to stop and pray about it together. We held hands in prayer—you know, like they ask you to do in church sometimes—and . . . man, oh man, I couldn't concentrate at all. All I could focus on was, "We're holding hands! We're holding hands! I'm in love!" When we got done, I told her we couldn't do that anymore. It was just too much for me. The "furthest" we went in our courtship was soft knucks—a very gentle and affectionate "pound it." The next time we held hands was when I proposed.

This brings up a very important scientific fact, and I say this sincerely: physical intimacy makes people stupid. Seriously, they lose all sense and self-control. People stay in horrible relationships because they are being physically intimate with their boyfriend or girlfriend. It is hard to see someone's complete lack of character when you are so preoccupied with them kissing you. Physical intimacy is exactly like the ball of fire we talked about earlier—it is *meant* to grow. A held hand is *meant* to give you a desire to hold that person close. Holding them close is *meant* to make you want to kiss them. It is all *meant* to escalate into a rapture of wonderful emotion and abandon. You're not meant to think or consider "where you should stop," you're meant to just go for it and enjoy each other. You're meant to let love awaken! Trying to have a "degree" of this is like trying to go up the first hill of a roller coaster and then asking the conductor to stop the cart. It's not supposed to work like that.

This biblical case is strongly supported by science. Studies demonstrate that even a light touch on the hand, arm, or shoulder brings about feelings of warmth and kindness toward the person who touched you.[3] Actions like holding hands have even stronger results. For example, one study demonstrated that women responded better to the threat of electric shock when they held hands with their husbands. The more satisfied they were in the relationship, the more pronounced this effect was. Tellingly, however, this

3. Hanzal et al., "The Role of Marital Status."

effect happened, although to a lesser degree, even if the women held hands with a stranger.[4] Another study demonstrated that someone who is being touched is more likely to comply with a request (for example, to buy something from a salesperson or to give something away for free).[5]

Physical touch chemically affects the way we think. One study demonstrated that pleasant touch of any sort, such as in hugging, produces oxytocin in the brains of the huggers, a chemical that makes each feel bonded to the other.[6] In the case of kissing, the effect is heightened. Lips are one to two hundred times more sensitive than fingertips, meaning kissing releases a *lot* of central nervous system endorphins and dopamine, in addition to increasing blood pressure and heart rate.[7] If you remember from health class, this is the same kind of response that happens when someone does drugs. That means when we kiss, we *feel good* and *want more*. It is *addictive*! And just like a drug addict will continue pursuing the substance that is ruining their life, kissing can keep you in an unhealthy relationship. It *bonds you* to the person you are kissing.

Of course, it's not just kissing. The types of touch that cause this "drug addict" response and the degree to which these responses occur seem to vary by gender. While women might interpret sitting on a lap, putting a leg over the partner's leg, and kissing as simply playful or affectionate, most men interpret them as purely sexual. Across both genders, however, being touched on the thigh, chest, and stomach (in addition to more obvious places) is statistically interpreted as sexual.[8] This means you are not "just" touching their thigh or their stomach or his chest. All of these actions are doing something to your brain chemistry that God intended for marriage alone.

4. Coan et al., "Lending a Hand," 1032
5. Gallace and Spence, "The Science of Interpersonal Touch."
6. Gallace and Spence, "The Science of Interpersonal Touch."
7. Alpert, "Philematology: The Science of Kissing," 466.
8. Hanzal et al., "The Role of Marital Status."

This all demonstrates that intimate physical touch—of *any* sort—bonds the two people who are touching. It also shows that intimate physical touch unhelpfully impedes your ability to thoughtfully evaluate the compatibility and character of the person you are courting. In fact, one surprising study reported that women place a very high value on their first kiss with their boyfriend. Literally, this study shows that if a great guy is a bad kisser, women tend to dump him.[9] What a croc! "Good" kissing is subjective and *learned.* There's a beautiful story of a man whose wife was paralyzed so that half of her face drooped. They could not kiss the way they always had. What did the husband do? He learned to drop part of his mouth so that their lips matched perfectly, and he could kiss her in the "right" way. *That's* the role kissing should play in a relationship: a demonstration of love, not a way to assess someone's worth as a spouse. But the aforementioned study indicates that this process happens *biologically.* In other words, she can't *help* that it affects the way she feels about him if he is not a good kisser. We should be wary of letting our "animal brain" be the decider for such things.[10]

By deciding to enter into a physical relationship, you are willingly interfering with your ability to wisely consider the things that are *really* important. Even a *little bit* of physicality in a relationship affects the nature of the relationship. It bonds you. It affects the way you think. We were *meant* to wait for physical relationships to flourish. If you are serious about courting for marriage and finding the best spouse possible, you cannot afford to be muddled in your thinking. There is a great safeguard built into courting because it requires involving others in the process, but it is easy to ignore wise counsel when you aren't thinking clearly.

Given all the evidence, it's plain that all physical acts are things that will affect the way you think and unhealthily promote intimacy outside of marriage. In other words, embracing physicality

9. Wlodarski and Dunbar, "Examining the Possible Functions of Kissing."

10. Wlodarski and Dunbar, "Examining the Possible Functions of Kissing."

in a relationship is both rejecting wisdom *and* embracing a sort of one-flesh bonding.

If you understand the seriousness of physicality in a relationship, then you will do well to protect yourself from temptation toward it. The first step is to decide what your standards will be. Obviously, I have made my position clear, but you must decide for yourself. All acts of physical intimacy should be categorized as "married" acts or "unmarried" acts—"things that I wouldn't mind telling a different spouse" or "things I would regret if I married someone else"—"things that would awaken love" or "things that are no big deal." So, you tell me, in what category does making out fall? Kissing on the lips in general? Kissing on the cheek? Holding hands?

The second step is to decide what you are willing to do to avoid physical temptation. Maybe it's best to be around others *as much as possible*. Maybe you two shouldn't watch a movie alone. Maybe you really *do* need to make a habit of "leaving room for Jesus." None of these are rules the Bible gives; they are rules you need to give yourself. They are rules that will protect both you and your courtship partner. You need to decide together which situations you can handle and which situations will lead to poor decisions with chemical consequences. I encourage you to think through this carefully and commit to specific standards. Whatever you decide, avoid the danger; flee temptation.[11]

REFLECTION QUESTIONS

1. Which physical boundaries do you think are best to have in place in a courting relationship? Consider committing to these in your Courting Commitments section in the back of the book.
2. What safeguards do you think are best to have in place to avoid breaching these physical boundaries?

11. 1 Corinthians 6:18

16

Emotional Unmarriage

What about protecting yourselves emotionally? How can you do that? Emotional boundaries have to do primarily with preventing unhealthy attachment. We've seen how this can happen through physical actions, but there are other concerns.

A healthy marriage is a committed relationship in which two people love each other and have shared themselves completely with each other. They *know* each other like no one else does. You get a glimpse of this truth when the Bible makes statements like, "Now Adam *knew* Eve his wife, and she conceived and bore Cain" (ESV).[1] Scripture, even in Hebrew (*yada*), links sex and marriage to truly *knowing* someone. Becoming one means knowing each other on the deepest emotional level. Again, this is meant to happen between two married people or not at all because, again, the Bible *implores* us to not awaken love before its time.

Emotionally, awakening love refers to the act of "falling in love." Unsurprisingly, science backs up the power and consequence of this emotional attachment. For example, the blood of people who are "in love" has lower levels of serotonin, a compound that, among other things, helps you think clearly. The effect can be

1. Genesis 4:1

unhealthy: one article describes how being "in love" can lead to obsessive behaviors—sometimes even to the levels of those with Obsessive Compulsive Disorder.[2] So, even without the physical aspects, emotional love can change the way we think. We cannot think calmly about the person we love in this way, and we may even obsess over them.

Interestingly, this same scientific article relates the feelings that accompany being "in love" with the feelings that cause the placebo effect (when a fake medicine, for example, is given to a patient, and their symptoms improve because they *think* they took real medicine). A placebo response and the experience of being "in love" both light up the limbic system (the "reward and pleasure" part of the brain) because there is an expectation that something good is about to happen.[3] But this means that, like the placebo effect, feeling "in love" *may* be inspired by something *other than the real thing.* In other words, you may *feel* like this person is a "one" when they are really *not*. Being "in love" has blinded you.

The overwhelming nature of being "in love" has been testified to in many cultures since ancient times. For example, ancient Egyptians called love "ensnaring," in marital and non-marital contexts. Ancient Mesopotamians compared love to wine. In one way or another, love has always been seen as "intoxicating."[4] And the Bible is no exception. For example, though Jacob had to work for seven years in order to marry Rachel, we are told that "they seemed like only a few days to him because of his love for her."[5] Song of Solomon 8:6–7 affirms, "[L]ove is as strong as death," and, "Many waters cannot quench love; rivers cannot sweep it away." Everyone knows it: the emotional experience of being "in love" is disruptive to the normal patterns of life.

It is for these reasons that while you are considering whether your courtship partner is the person you want to marry, you should

2. Esch and Stefano, "The Neurobiology of Love," 184.

3. Esch and Stefano, "The Neurobiology of Love," 180–81.

4. Keener and Walton, NKJV Cultural Backgrounds Study Bible, 1126–27.

5. Genesis 29:20

not let unhealthy emotional attachment infest your relationship. It would be impossible to keep all disruptive excitement and feelings of affection out of the relationship, but you should not invite in any more of it than is natural when spending time with someone you think you might marry. (This does not mean avoiding making memories and enjoying each other's company—that is the mark of any friendship!)

So, what do you think? Does going to the skating rink together lead to unhealthy emotional attachment and prematurely awakened love? What about going on a trip with a group of friends? Going on a trip with your family? Hanging out alone in a basement? What about texting them all day? Texting them into the night? Sharing deep personal secrets? Telling them you love them? Making life plans together? Naming babies together? Sharing a bed? Celebrating anniversaries? Where do you draw the line?

Unhealthy emotional intimacy brings heartbreak when a relationship ends. Such a relationship is not *innocent* and *honorable,* like Boaz and Ruth's was; it is unhealthily committed. It creates fractured souls because each soul has emotionally bonded with the other beyond the point of friendship. It is not wise, and it is not God's best for a relationship.

Kylie and I practiced healthy emotional boundaries as much as possible when we were courting. We seldom hung out alone. And when we did, it was almost always outside and where other people were able to see us. We would even plan ahead so that if we were hanging out indoors with a friend, and we knew a friend was going to leave, we had a specific outdoor location in mind to go to. In retrospect, though, perhaps no area of our courtship reveals these boundaries more than our texting relationship.

Kylie still has the phone she had when we courted years ago. In the process of writing this book, I have been able to revisit every text we sent each other from the night I got her number to the afternoon before I asked her to marry me (and beyond). Though it's personal, I am convinced that sharing some information about these texts and some of the texts themselves will benefit some of you. First, there were several trends in our texting. We texted each other an average of 18 times a day in our courtship (not counting my time in India). We texted each other the most on Fridays and Saturdays: about 27 times on those days. The time we texted each other the most in our relationship was before we were even courting: an average of 22 or 23 texts every day, with as many as 61 texts in a day. In courtship, our record was 50 texts in a day (followed by 44, then 43).

The opposite was also true. There were several days, before and during courtship, when we didn't text each other at all. Of the sixty-eight days we could have texted each other, there were a total of eleven days that we texted each other 4 times or less. These days were typically days when we were hanging out with other people. At noon, I would tell Kylie I was hanging out with my family, and then I wouldn't text her again until 10 PM. The time she went on a trip with my sister to Colorado, we hardly texted at all. In fact, I would say we consistently tried to refrain from texting each other if at all possible. Hence, the following texting conversation from August 3, 2017:

> K: 3:28 PM
> *We definitely need to chat. I feel like so much has happened in the last day!!!*

> Z: 3:32 PM
> Lol, I've been feeling that since yesterday morning.

So, numerically speaking, we didn't feel the need to talk to each other every day. We practiced healthy boundaries by saying, "I don't need to text him/her right now. I need to focus on the person in front of me." We did not prioritize each other over everyone else in our lives.

More important than any of this, though, was the content of our texts. If I had to put a number on it, I would say that 80–85 percent of our texts had to do with Jesus in some way: a Bible verse, an encouragement, a prayer request. A lot of the rest was logistics: "When do you get off work?" "Are you still awake?" "Can I call you later? How does 7:00 work?"

But of course, there was also *other* stuff. And in these texts, we were definitely affectionate and kind, but squeaky clean in every regard to where I'm not embarrassed to share them. In fact, here are some examples of what we said to each other over text, only lightly edited (to conceal our friends' and families' identities and whatnot—it seemed like the right thing to do). These next four are from before we were courting:

Wednesday, 04/26/17 (this is the first text I sent Kylie after getting her number):

> Z: 10:55 PM
> This is a test text! Jesus loves you so so much! He is your sabbath and your true rest regardless of how you sleep tonight! I'll be praying for you :)

Friday, 04/28/17 (just a few days before officially courting):

K: 8:59 PM
Guess what

> Z: 9:00 PM
> What?
> Z: 9:19 PM
> What what

9:21 PM
*K: Chicken b**t. Wanna go on a walk?*

> Z: 9:22 PM
> Fo shizzle :)

Later that night (in preparation for going country dancing):

> Z: 11:14 PM
> Hey, [your roommate] said you're the mastermind behind the fancy dance Sunday night. Where would the location be for this event?

K: 11:18 PM
So you're staying potentially maybe hopefully? It's at the Eagles but I've never been so we might need to get some deets

Z: 11:38 PM
Hopefully maybe I might Lord willing stay, yes. :) And groovy, idk about [our friends] but I think it might be a double d**e :)

K: 11:49 PM
That would rock my sox off

Z: 11:57 PM
Same :)

And finally, Sunday, 04/30/17:

Z: 10:03 AM
Hey, I need to tell you the Lord is putting it on my heart and told us three times in His word (Song of Songs 2:7, 3:5, AND 8:4) that we "not rouse or awaken love until it so desires." I want to honor God and enjoy this season to the max! So I'm reading this Desiring God article about those verses and it's pretty rock and roll. It says Song of Solomon "depicts and praises the breathtaking intensity of a unique, lifelong, committed relationship between one man and one woman—what we might call, 'friendship on fire.'" That sounds pretty phenomenal and I really want to seek that in the Lord with you. Seek first His kingdom and its righteousness and all these things will be added unto you! :D

K: 10:04 AM
Zach

Z: 10:05 AM
Yes'm?

K: 10:14 AM
That's perfect. And it confirms what God has been telling me

And so it went! After our courtship was officially established, our texts often looked something like this exchange:

Tuesday, 05/02/17:

> Z: 11:03 PM
> Jesus loves you so much! You are so so precious in His sight! Have a wunderbar nacht y mucho paz, homegirl!

K: 11:18 PM
Thank you for always bringing Jesus to the center :) I feel that inexplicable peace again :) How would you define courting?

Or this one, from Sunday, 05/14/17:

K: 10:38 AM
Yo yo yo what's the plan, stan?

> Z: 10:44 AM
> First, we praise Jesus while I drive to your place. Then we praise Jesus in one of our cars on the way to church! And we praise Him all morning! Thoughts?

K: 10:44 AM
Perfecto. Vamos

> Z: 10:47 AM
> stage 1 initiated

But of course, there were times we told each other how we felt about each other. Notice in each of these examples, though, how we consistently steered it back toward Jesus and toward "*The Zone of Healthy Emotional Attachment.*"

Check out this one from Tuesday, 05/09/17:

> Z: 5:59 PM
> I'm really excited to hear about your day! I've been resisting the urge to be on my phone, it's a lot harder than it used to be for some reason . . .

K: 6:10 PM
I'm really excited to hear your voice! Oh my goodness, Zach . . . two months . . . eazy peazy. (referencing my trip to India)

Z: 6:15 PM
for sure! I think I can already tell how much it'll put God at the very center, I'm pretty pumped about that :)

This one is where Kylie instituted our "Nah" rule: when you want to say something that's *definitely* crossing the line in terms of intimacy, you just say, "Nah," instead. Hence, 05/11/17:

K: 6:03 PM
Hey, Zach?

Z: 6:21 PM
Yes?

K: 6:26 PM
Nah :) see ya soon, Lord willing

Z: 6:27 PM
Ha-ha sounds good :)

In retrospect, I might classify this one as a (pretty darn innocent) slip-up. Friday, 05/12/17:

K: 12:16 AM
Iyq (meaning, I like you)

Z: 7:10 AM
iyq2

K: 7:28 AM
:) :) :)

As our relationship deepened, it became harder to hold back from saying things that we shouldn't. It is essential to keep up the good fight, especially in those moments.

Sunday, 07/23/17:

K: 7:03 PM
Zach, I miss ya, man. Is this normal???

Z: 7:03 PM
Ha-ha, is what normal?

K: 7:17 PM
To miss you this much

Z: 7:24 PM
Couldn't say for sure, but the feeling is reciprocated, my dear :)

K: 8:00 PM
That is such a modest and beautiful word of affection. Are you home yet?

Friday, 07/28/17 (back and neck rubs and scratches are common practice in my childhood home):

Z: 11:37 PM
I could only do this for my wife, but how do you feel about back and neck rubs and scratches?
Z: 11:39 PM
Is that weird to ask?
I feel like that was a little weird to ask

K: 11:40 PM
Maybe just something to ask your wife. So if that is ever my role I will let you know then :)

Z: 11:41 PM
Groovy, thank you for your grace :)

And, as a very last example, a couple of days before our engagement, Thursday, 08/31/17:

Z: 7:40 AM
I am quite fond of you Miss V. And I'm just thinking how God makes our affection seem tiny. So He is ridiculously nuts about you and definitely can't stop thinking about you . . . ever! It is a beautiful morning! Happy day, Ky :)

K: 10:50 AM
Mister, that was quite the message to wake up to this morning :) It actually really opened my eyes to how much He truly, truly loves us. He thinks about you more than I do!!! That's insane. I pray His love shines through to those children and their purity to you. JOYOUS day, Zachary :)

* * *

So, as you've now seen, sometimes Kylie slipped into "Lovesville" and sometimes I did. It took the both of us to make our relationship as pure as it was. In all of these conversations, not once did we say those "three magic words." We were not crossing the emotional boundaries we put in place for ourselves. Physical and emotional boundaries are key to having a healthy courtship. What are yours?

REFLECTION QUESTIONS

1. What do you think of the texting trends mentioned in this chapter? Do you text your friends (or do the equivalent) more or less than Zach and Kylie texted each other in courtship? What do you think is a healthy average for yourself?
2. What do you think about the language in the texts sampled in this chapter? What aspects of the language would you want to emulate?
3. Which emotional boundaries do you think are best to have in place in a courting relationship? Consider committing to these in your Courting Commitments section in the back of the book.
4. What safeguards do you think are best to have in place to avoid breaching these emotional boundaries?

17

Spiritual Unmarriage, Plus

Finally, we need to consider spiritual boundaries. This category is the most straightforward and the least lengthy. We'll go over it and then conclude with thoughts on the great blessings of acting unmarried.

A spiritual life exists primarily between an individual and God. However, there is a part of a spiritual life that can also be shared with others. This happens when we confess sin to each other, when we pray together, and when we talk vulnerably about our relationships with God. All of these things are meant to happen frequently in a marriage. But, again, when it comes to the opposite sex, that level of spiritual intimacy should be achieved within the context of marriage or not at all.

How long would you consider praying with a "normal" friend of the opposite sex, particularly alone? How much would you confess to them? Would you have them as an accountability partner? Would you make a point to stop going to your church so you can go to theirs? These actions connect people. They create unhealthy attachments if they are not founded in a loving, permanent relationship. Like physical and emotional intimacy, it is unwise to foster spiritual intimacy before its time.

The wisdom of courting with these physical, emotional, and spiritual boundaries is confirmed in so many ways. For example, if you court within these boundaries, then you are truly practicing for marriage; the way you act toward members of the opposite sex *before* you are married is identical to the way you will *after*. Think about it: would it be okay for me to hold hands, cuddle, kiss, or do something more with a woman other than Kylie? People call that an affair. Would it be okay for me to become best friends with another woman and spend an abundance of alone time with her? People call that an emotional affair. Would it be okay for me to intentionally go to another woman's church or join her small group? Would it be okay to study Scripture alone and pray for extended periods of time with her? I don't know what people call that, but it'd be weird. I would never do these things with another woman because she is not my wife! If you court this way, you will be prepared to be married this way. (As a side note, I think the fact that these boundaries are obvious in marriage tells us something about the kind of relationship these acts are intended for.)

Courting with these boundaries also leads to great security in marriage. If the person you marry has controlled themself from being physically, emotionally, and spiritually intimate with anyone but you, there is so much less worry that they will be unfaithful. They have saved themself for you, their spouse, alone. They have decided that *you* and *you alone* were worth it. They have no one else in mind when they are with you. What a gift and what security. Not to mention, what a lack of potential jealousy. You are their true one and only!

Finally, courting with these boundaries leads to security and joy, even if you *don't* get married. Think of an average breakup in a dating relationship. Nine times out of ten, the two people involved don't want to see or talk to each other again, at least for a long while. And the more intimacy there was, the more heartbreak there is, and the less they want to remember the other person at all. There are serious *scars*. A courting relationship does not have to be that way. You have not been physically intimate. You have not intertwined your lives. You have stayed separate, thought through things clearly, and come to the conclusion that the two of you just aren't a good match for marriage. Ideally, if you have selected a wise person who is on the same page as to the purpose of courting, the breakup will be mutual. Two mature courters can walk away from their courtship and have a real possibility of still being friends. If you broke up with the person you are courting, would you be able to stay friends? Would you be able to tell your future spouse everything about your relationship? Would your future spouse be jealous, or would they appreciate how you courted? Think through these things before you get into a situation you regret.

REFLECTION QUESTIONS

1. Does the fruit of acting unmarried, spoken of in this chapter, affect your attitude toward the boundaries proposed in the last several chapters? If so, how?
2. Which spiritual boundaries do you think are best to have in place in a courting relationship? Consider committing to these in your Courting Commitments section in the back of the book.
3. What safeguards do you think are best to have in place to avoid breaching these spiritual boundaries?

18

Pulling Back the Reins

In response to these last chapters, I know some of you have a single thought going through your mind: "*It's too late*." What are you supposed to do if you have already "crossed the line"? What if you have already become intimate—physically, emotionally, or spiritually? The answer to these questions depends on what specifically has happened and in what category you have "crossed the line," but in general, there are two options: back off or break up.

Let's say you and your courtship partner have already become spiritually intimate. Maybe you have been accountability partners for the last several months, and now you have decided that you shouldn't have been. What should you do? To put it simply, you probably just need to back off. Intimacy that has already happened cannot be taken back, and breaking up certainly won't make it go away any more than just stopping will. If you think your actions and decisions have been sinful or foolish, then repent, ask God for forgiveness and wisdom, and live out your courtship according to your new convictions from this point forward. The only reason you should break up with your courtship partner in moments like these is if they are not willing to make the change. If this is the case, you are breaking up because they are showing their true colors; they are not a race partner of equal "height" and "speed," and therefore they are not a good match for marriage.

The same approach is probably proper if there has been emotional intimacy in the relationship. Maybe you and your courtship partner have already named your future babies, and now you think that wasn't such a good idea. What do you do? Well, don't name any more. Back off, but probably don't break up. Again, maybe the only reason to break up in this case would be if your courtship partner doesn't think it was a big deal, or if they try to continue coming up with names. Again, you're getting a glimpse of their heart and priorities if that's the case, and maybe, as a result, you'll talk to a good mentor and decide together that they are not a good match for marriage after all. Maybe this will not be the conclusion, but it certainly could be. It'll be a bummer to have decided-on baby names floating around in your head when you are married to a different person, but it will be better than marrying less than God's best.

Of course, there are many different kinds of situations in the spiritual and emotional intimacy realms, but these examples of "crossing the line," by being accountability partners or by naming babies, provide good guidelines to help you think through the specific situation you find yourself in.

Now for the big one. What do you do if you have crossed the line physically? It is right to call this category "the big one"; as 1 Corinthians 6:18 makes clear, sexual sin is more serious than other kinds of sin: "All other sins a person commits are outside the body, but whoever sins sexually, sins against their own body." This means that your response to crossing the line physically might need to be more extreme than if you have crossed it spiritually or emotionally. The proper response depends on exactly what has happened. Have you held hands, and now you want to stop? That probably calls for one response. Have you had sex? That probably calls for another. And what if you've gotten pregnant? That is something else entirely.

Let's take each of these scenarios as representative situations, dealing with one at a time. What should you do if you have held hands, or done other intimate activities that stop short of sex? Assuming you really want to stop (remember, holding hands isn't necessarily a sin, but I think it's clearly unwise), your response *may* be similar to what it would be for crossing the line spiritually or emotionally: backing off, and only breaking up if it is clear that they are not someone you want to marry. When it comes to physical intimacy, however, it probably won't be that simple. It's a lot easier to stop naming future babies together than it is to stop kissing, for example. And even though kissing isn't listed as a sin in the Bible, it can still leave some major emotional scars. This means that the stakes are higher and the brakes are harder to effectively stomp.

If you are serious about stopping, you might have to take serious measures. First Corinthians 6:18 exhorts us with these four simple words: "Flee from sexual immorality." The perfect example of this verse in action comes from Genesis 39. Potiphar's wife, a married Egyptian woman, decides that her husband ain't cuttin' it anymore. So, behind his back, she repeatedly approaches Joseph to get him to sleep with her. Verses 12–13 read, "One day [Joseph] went into the house to attend to his duties, and none of the household servants was inside. [Potiphar's wife] caught him by his cloak and said, 'Come to bed with me!' *But he left his cloak in her hand and ran out of the house*" (emphasis mine). Joseph wanted to get away from sexual immorality, even if it meant fleeing outside half-naked. He was willing to take serious measures.

In the Sermon on the Mount, Jesus encourages the same kind of seriousness when it comes to sexual sin: "If your right eye causes you to stumble, gouge it out and throw it away. It is better for you to lose one part of your body than for your whole body to be thrown into hell. And if your right hand causes you to stumble, cut it off and throw it away. It is better for you to lose one part of your body than for your whole body to go into hell."[1] Jesus is exaggerating on purpose here, but his point is clear: do whatever it takes to avoid sexual immorality.

If you really want to stop holding hands—or kissing, or whatever it is you want to stop—what are you willing to do to make it

1. Matthew 5:29–30

happen? If you have not done it very much, you might be able to stop by just committing to it, like Kylie and I did after holding hands to pray. But if you have done a lot of it, especially if it's something like kissing, you might need to call for reinforcements. The "level one" step would be to talk about it with someone you trust and make them your accountability partner. Have them check in on you two regularly, maybe over the phone or maybe dropping by in person. This kind of accountability is irreplaceable if you want to stop whatever you're doing. A "level two" step, if you're really struggling, would be to have multiple accountability partners and to never hang out without them. You might think of this option as the equivalent of Joseph running out of the room half-naked—a little excessive-seeming, but definitely no regrets afterward. As time goes on, you might decide to just *seldom* hang out without your accountability partners; just remember, purity is worth the effort.

The "level three" option, depending on just how serious you are, would be to break up, at least for a short time. You might think of this as the "cutting off your hand" option. If you cannot seem to stop being physically intimate, and you are meeting up with your courtship partner without telling your accountability partners, you may decide that this drastic measure is worth it. It will give each of you time to refocus on God and give you enough clarity of thought to re-engage righteously when you're ready. Talk about the options with your courtship partner, perhaps with a mentor there as well, and poke your eye out if need be.

What about if you have had sex, maybe multiple times? The Old Testament is most helpful on this issue. Exodus 22:16–17 says, "If a man seduces a virgin who is not pledged to be married and sleeps with her, he must pay the bride-price, and she shall be his wife. If her father absolutely refuses to give her to him, he must still pay the bride-price for virgins." There are obviously some cultural differences at play in these verses, but the main topic is exactly what we are discussing here: consensual premarital sex. According to these verses, if a man has premarital sex with a woman, he gives the woman's father money, and the father makes the call on whether the two get married or not.

It'd be easy to laugh this off as outdated, except for the fact that it comes from the perfect law of God,[2] not the Code of Hammurabi. Then again, it is also from the Old Testament, and don't we get to ignore some of those commands? Answering this will require a bit of an extended tangent.

It is true that the Old Testament Law is no longer binding on Christians.[3] This essentially means that, unless it is explicitly repeated in the New Testament, we are not necessarily obligated to follow an Old Testament commandment. This commandment regarding consensual premarital sex is nowhere repeated in the New Testament, and so it would make sense to conclude we can ignore it. But we must be more careful than that in determining whether it should hold any sway over our decision-making.

There is a difference between what is sometimes called the *letter* of Old Testament laws and the *abiding principle* of the Old Testament laws. Consider the laws of avoiding pork,[4] avoiding shellfish,[5] and not mixing linen and wool in garments.[6] To follow the *letter* of these laws would mean abstaining from what they literally *say*: no bacon cheeseburgers, no seafood buffets, and no blended fabrics. To follow the *abiding principle* of these laws would mean seeking to understand the deeper reason these particular laws existed—what they are really *getting at*—and abiding by that *principle* instead of the letter. For example, the principle behind not eating pork and shellfish and not mixing linen and wool was holiness: these practices made the Israelites distinct from the rest of the world, as God's people, and symbolically "pure." If we are seeking to follow the *abiding principle* of these laws, then we will be holy and distinct and abstain from worldliness and sin, but we will not necessarily abstain from eating bacon or wearing polyblends.

2. See, e.g., Romans 7:12
3. Romans 10:4; Galatians 3:23–25; Ephesians 2:15
4. Leviticus 11:7–8; Deuteronomy 14:8
5. Leviticus 11:9–12; Deuteronomy 14:9–10
6. Leviticus 19:19; Deuteronomy 22:11

As Jesus exemplified[7] and God confirmed,[8] Christians *are* to observe the abiding principles of the Law, though they do not need to abide by the letter.[9]

Of course, for some laws, there is no difference between the letter and the abiding principle. For example, Exodus 20:13 says, "You shall not murder." What is the abiding principle behind this law? That human life is precious, and that only God has the ultimate authority to take it. In this case, following the abiding principle of the law actually goes beyond the letter,[10] but it still obviously includes not murdering, just like the letter of the law says. We can put all Old Testament laws through this process and decide whether the abiding principle matches the letter or not.

So, what's the abiding principle of this law about premarital sex? And does it match the letter? Understanding some cultural facts may help us determine the answer. In order for a man to marry a woman in ancient Israel, he would have to pay her father a bride-price. A daughter who lost her virginity would not be as valuable in the eyes of men in that culture. They would either not have married her, or they would have only paid a smaller bride-price for her. This means that the father would lose some financial security because of the premarital sex that took place.[11] This loss in the woman's status would also make it difficult for the woman to marry another man in the future.

So, it seems this law did many things: First, as seen more clearly in the parallel law in Deuteronomy 22:28–29, it provided for the father's financial loss by making the man pay him fifty shekels of silver (equivalent to several years' wages[12]). Second, it served to protect the woman from her likely fate of singleness by requiring the man to marry her.[13] Finally, both the bride-price

7. See, e.g., Matthew 5; Luke 10:25–37

8. See, e.g., Acts 10

9. See also, e.g., 1 Corinthians 9:9–10; 1 Timothy 5:17–18

10. See Matthew 5:21–22

11. Keener and Walton, NKJV Cultural Backgrounds Study Bible, 156.

12. ESV Study Bible, 180.

13. ESV Study Bible, 363.

and the forced marriage would serve to provide for the potential child born from the union.[14]

What then does it mean to follow the abiding principle of this law? *At the very least*, this law teaches us that we are obligated to take responsibility for our actions and that we are also obligated, in certain situations, to make up for any damage we cause others, especially in a sexual relationship.

Applying the abiding principle of this law to a modern situation where you and your courtship partner have had sex is a little tricky, however. In our culture, if two people have premarital sex, the father is not out of any money, and neither person in the situation will probably have trouble finding another spouse if things don't work out between them. Do you need to take responsibility for your actions? Absolutely. Is it best to follow the letter of the law and get married? I don't think we can use this law to say that. What's at stake in the ancient versus the modern setting is simply too different. In other words, the abiding principle of the law seems to leave room for staying single after having premarital sex since those involved are not as affected as they would have been in ancient times. And certainly, the letter of the law indicates that choosing to stay single was an option (if the father refused to allow his daughter to marry the man).

Putting everything together, then, though it is ideal to be sexually intimate with only one person in your life, it might be the case that those involved (the two of you, as well as the wise mentors and pastors you need to ask for advice in this situation) decide that it is *really* not a good idea for you two to get married, in which case you should not.

This is, of course, a very big decision. First Corinthians 6:15–16 makes it clear that in having sex, two unmarried people have unnaturally participated in what was only meant to exist in the one-flesh relationship of marriage. This means deciding to break up will come with hurt and baggage. Perhaps because of this, you all will decide that the best thing to do is to continue courting and at least consider marriage. If this is the route you

14. Keener and Walton, NKJV Cultural Backgrounds Study Bible, 347.

choose, the options to avoid repeating the same mistake are exactly the same as with holding hands or kissing (levels one, two, and three), but the measures should be more drastic than just the two of you committing to stopping. You need accountability, and you almost definitely also need the constant presence of accountability partners when you're together, at least for a long while. You may decide, as well, to take a break in order to refocus on God and renew your relationship with him. Remember, *that* relationship is far more important than any other. Whatever you decide, repent, ask for forgiveness from God and from each other, and commit to making the change.

Finally, let's address what you should do if you get pregnant. I use the plural "you" here because, if this happens, you are *both* going to end up with a child. In this situation, you are in a very similar boat to the previous scenario of having premarital sex without getting pregnant. Of course, the consequences are more severe with a child involved, but based on the Exodus verses, the reality seems to be the same: it is probably better for you two to be married; however, you and others also might decide that you *really* shouldn't. And again, maybe you need to continue courting to find out which is the case. Obviously, it is going to be hard any way you do it. And even more than in the previous scenario, you are both going to have to take responsibility for your actions and do your best to make up for the damages done. Assuming you are not putting the baby up for adoption—adoption being an option that should be prayed about and talked about at great length, with pastors and other wise counselors heavily involved—taking responsibility means you should both support the child financially. It means, if at all possible, you should both be in the child's life. And it means, maybe more than anything else, that you both need to humbly ask for a *lot* of support from those around you for the days and years ahead. You will need good godly counsel, and lots of it. Whatever route you choose, remember that, if you love and are following God, he can work even this for your good *and* the child's.

If you have messed up in terms of intimacy—spiritually, emotionally, or physically, to *any* degree—please understand that it is *not* too late. It is not too late to make a change; it is not too late to have a healthy courtship; and it is not too late to be forgiven. Our God delights to give grace upon grace upon grace. He is a good and mighty God, overflowing with compassion for his children. He will not despise you if you come with a repentant heart.[15] Trust him. Ask for his help and strength. Believe that he gives beauty for ashes. Delight in him, and he will give you the desires of your heart.

As we conclude this section of the book, I'd like to give you some "tips and tricks" that I've gathered over the years—some policies that Kylie and I had in place while we were courting and some policies we still have in place today in order to protect our purity.

First, have a mindset not of "how much can we do," but "how pure can we stay." A relationship should not revolve around the idea that "sex outside of marriage is sin, so *that's* the thing to avoid." It should revolve around the idea that intimacy outside of marriage is foolish, so any form of it should be avoided, if possible. Remember, you are first and foremost Christ's, and you are spending a lifetime preparing to be with him. Fight to be as pure as possible.

Second, as Scripture encourages, guard your hearts.[16] In Scripture, the heart is the center of a person's decisions and affections. A heart that has become unhealthy or damaged will have a hard time loving what it is supposed to or making the decisions it should. That means that with everyone you interact with, but especially a courtship partner, make sure you are guarding your own and the other person's heart. Protect it from becoming unhealthily attached and risking scars that will forever affect future decisions and affections. The heart is a precious thing, and you don't want to be responsible for hurting someone else's.

Third, stay public and vertical. Having this rule specified makes it really easy to avoid falling into temptation. It's easy to kiss someone when no one else is around. It's easy to make mistakes when you're lying down together, especially at night when your self-control is impaired. Remaining public and vertical keeps all

15. Psalm 51:17

16. Proverbs 4:23

of that out of the question. By the way, staying public is a policy Kylie and I still follow with other members of the opposite sex—it not only avoids any possible temptations, but also leaves no room for suspicion from others about whether inappropriate activities are going on. Boaz certainly cared about how the relationship appeared to other people.[17] So should you.

Fourth, really consider whether the guy should pay for the gal's meals. Seriously. Guys, how often do you buy your friends' food for them? That's how often you should pay for your courtship partner. I *rarely* bought Kylie's meals for her while we were courting. There was something about it that healthily reminded us that we were still two individuals, and not yet one flesh. That wasn't my role yet. I was not her provider. Obviously, many people would disagree with me on this one, but it's something at least worth considering.

Fifth, master the side hug. I'm a hugger. Side hugs are an easy way to protect hearts and avoid any misunderstandings by spectators or anyone else.

Dating is not meant to *be* marriage; it is meant to *seek* marriage. If you want someone cute who you enjoy being around and spending a ton of time with, who you can stay up late talking to, who you can hug and kiss and do whatever you want with . . . that's called marriage. Don't let dating rob it of its beauty. You are designed to do all these things for the rest of your life with your spouse *in security*. You are meant to experience that fun and vulnerability in the stability of a relationship with someone who has agreed never to leave.

Courting is for something different. At its best, courting is meant to be (putting together the pieces of this book) a process of considering marriage—between two people who are ready for marriage, who love Jesus, and who see in each other possible equal yoking, similar racing qualities, and godly character—supported and advised by wise counselors and kept free of physical, emotional, and spiritual intimacy.

17. See Ruth 3:14

In other words, courting is the consideration of marriage between two *friends*. Lord willing, you will enter a courtship as friends and remain that way throughout the courtship process. And when this process ends in a lifelong commitment, courting is like two live wires approaching each other, both coursing with energy. In courtship, the two "wires" assess, "*Is this the kind of spark that God wants for me?*" They decide it is. They get engaged. The wires grow closer. The anticipation builds. Longing. Excitement. Closer. And closer. And closer! Until—*CONTACT!* Marriage. Electricity. That kind of electric marriage is just what a courtship leads to when the people involved are willing to act unmarried.

REFLECTION QUESTIONS

1. If you are in a relationship, have you breached any emotional or spiritual boundaries that you need to rein in? Based on the advice offered in this chapter, how should you do so?
2. If you are in a relationship, have you breached any physical boundaries? What level of response do these call for?
3. What advice and encouragement would you give to a friend who is ashamed that they had sex or got pregnant with their courtship partner?

19

Shooting It Straight

RELATIONSHIPS OF ANY KIND are delicate. Though courting avoids much of the unnecessary attachment dating breeds, attachment on some level is inevitable. And when fallen humans are in such a vulnerable, delicate relationship, letting each other discover who they really are, it is easy to want to protect the other person's feelings at all costs. You see some concerns in the other person, or you are bothered by something they do, but so they don't feel bad, you don't say what probably needs to be said. Or, on the other hand, *you* are insecure about something, you want to protect yourself from feeling bad, and so you try to manipulate the other person into treating you a certain way.

Many people in relationships play these relationship games: dropping "hints" and telling half-truths on one end; giving the silent treatment, withholding affection, flirting with others to make the other person jealous, threatening to break up, or breaking up so they chase after you on the other. These games then breed suspicion and sometimes blatant lying. "*Does she really mean that?*" "*Does he really like me?*" None of this is God's will; he does not want you to play games, manipulate each other, or lie to each other, even to protect your own feelings or the other person's. He wants you to be authentic and honest.

Look at Boaz and Ruth's story again. Do you notice how straightforward they were with each other? Nowhere is this more clearly seen than in the actual "proposal scene" from Ruth 3. When Ruth got prettied up and approached Boaz, there was absolutely no doubt about her intentions: she wanted him to marry her. It was impossible for him to misinterpret what she was doing. He responded in kind, telling her very clearly that he would, if possible, marry her the very next day. He made the sincerity of his words clear by then giving her a generous gift. All of this led Naomi to observe that Boaz meant business—he would not rest until the deed was resolved.

This was a mutual, straightforward pursuit of a relationship, without indecency. Boaz and Ruth were not using each other, manipulating each other, or wasting each other's time. Ruth could have played hard to get. Instead of plainly initiating a proposal, she could have pulled back from Boaz, trying to get him to somehow realize that she was interested in marrying him. She could have dropped "subtle" hints. Boaz, likewise, could have made vague promises about marrying her "one day." He could have tried to dodge her question, or made a joke out of it, or responded with a perpetual, "Not yet." None of these was the case; Boaz and Ruth were consistently serious and upfront about what they each were doing.

As soon as what Boaz promised had happened, he told everyone that Ruth was his. He did this at the town's gate, which was essentially a combined town hall and courthouse, where elders witnessed transactions and decided cases.[1] This was a *public* and *legal* commitment. He followed through on what he had said he would do. He wasn't playing games.

Relationships of any sort lead to hurt when two people aren't straightforward and honest with each other. Be careful of falling prey to game-playing. Make it clear you aren't messing around. No

1. See Deuteronomy 21:19; 22:15; 25:7; 2 Samuel 15:2; Job 29:7–17; Proverbs 22:22; 31:23; Amos 5:10

playing hard to get. No trying to make them jealous. No making them play the guessing game.

This principle manifests itself differently in different stages of the relationship. First of all, boys, if you like a girl enough to consider courting her, and you've done your research on her, then tell her! Though a boyfriend is not the head of his girlfriend in the same way a husband is of his wife, it is still proper for the man to initiate the courting relationship. A courtship led by the woman will have a rough time transitioning to a marriage led by the man. So, be a man and make the first unambiguous move.

Ladies, in the same way, you ought to give an unambiguous response, though avoid initiating a relationship, per se. It is tempting to see Ruth's action at the threshing floor as one of initiation, not responsiveness. Thinking carefully about it, however, it is clear that she is primarily showing herself as available. She had been in mourning, and she was now clearly expressing her interest in marriage, but she was not proposing; she let Boaz do the actual pursuing in the moment.

The lesson here, ladies, is that if you are interested in a boy, and you've checked out his character from afar, it is good to present yourself as clearly single and ready to mingle. Don't shut yourself up in a cloister hoping he'll come find you. Don't endlessly flirt with him or pretend to like another boy to make him jealous; have a real conversation with him. Again, I'm *not* proposing you say, "Hey, I've heard a lot about you. Please court me!" Just talk to him! And as things develop, if you feel a mutual pull toward courting, it's probably appropriate to invite a pursuit if necessary: "Fred, do you like me?" You may think that only a guy should do this kind of thing, and that's okay. I think, though, ladies, you are okay to at least bring up the topic. It is a winsome invitation and could save you a few weeks (or months) of waiting and wondering. Either way, don't play games with each other. Be straightforward and protect each other's hearts. Communicate your intentions very clearly, and expect a very clear response.

Which leads me to my next point. If you aren't interested when someone approaches you, it is best to be clear about it.

"Shannon, that's very kind, but I don't feel that way about you." Clear honesty can sting a little, but it is infinitely better than masking the truth with bologna.

As you move into the context of a courtship, your intentions should remain clear. And your honesty should be a defining characteristic of your relationship. You are trying to get to know each other to discover if you should be together for the rest of your lives. It is cruel to not be candid. If it is important to you that your spouse be willing to move overseas, then you need to have an honest conversation about that before you decide to get married. And if your courtship partner asks you about something like that and you have always had a heart for rural Missouri, you need to tell them that very simply: "James, I love that you are so invested in the mission field abroad. Honestly, I've always seen myself living on a farm." Shoot it straight.

This kind of honesty is refreshing and beneficial on so many levels. Of course, the content of their answers will help you accurately decide if you should marry them. But honesty also creates a culture of openness and trust in the relationship. It avoids frustration and annoyance. For me, it was exceedingly helpful to be able to ask Kylie, "Is there anything wrong?" and expect a simple and honest yes or no. No games, no immaturity, just the truth. That is the kind of relationship you want.

Throughout this process with someone, one of two things will eventually happen. First, you may decide to end the courtship. This will happen when you have learned enough to know that the other person is not a good fit for you in marriage. As stated previously, this decision will ideally be mutual, but that will not always be the case. Sometimes, they will be disillusioned.

If you are leaning toward ending the relationship, honesty is still more important than anything else. Depending on the reason, it may be best to have a candid discussion before deciding whether to end the relationship or to end it straight away. A candid conversation might be something like, "Abby, I am still bothered that we don't see eye-to-eye on secular music. I really just don't want my kids listening to it. Have you thought any more about our discussion?" Maybe she responds, "Yes, I've thought about it, Jack, and I think you are actually right." Or maybe she says, "I haven't really decided yet." Or maybe, "Yes, Jack, I've thought about it, and I really don't think secular music is harmful as a rule. I don't think I would be able to not share with my kids some of my favorite songs I sang with my dad growing up." If Jack really cares about it, he needs to say, "Abby, I respect that it is a matter of personal conviction, and I know that wouldn't be a deal breaker for a lot of people, but it is a big deal to me. I think you are a great person, and I enjoy spending time with you, but I do not think we should get married."

An example of ending a relationship straight away, without any need for an extended conversation, might go something like, "Abby, I saw you kiss Jake. I am not okay with that, and I am not going to continue in this relationship." She might say something like, "I'm sorry! It was a mistake! It won't happen again!" to which he should respond, "Abby, you've lost my trust, and I will not marry someone I can't trust. Goodbye." There is no explanation that should make you stay in a relationship with someone who is clearly not interested in giving you the kind of love that God wants in marriage.

As stated in chapter 13, if you decide it is best to end a relationship, you need to tell your partner as soon as you know. If it's a character issue that you have seen repeated evidence of, I don't recommend there being a conversation about how "they need to change if you are going to stay in the relationship." You never want to be the reason that your courtship partner is pursuing righteousness. They need to change because they want to change before *God*, not before *you*.

So, what should *that* conversation look like? Perhaps something like this: "I want to tell you something hard—I think it is best we end our courtship. I have thought and prayed a lot about it, and I've gotten counsel on it, and there are some things that I think would make a marriage together not work." At that point, it's important that you tell them clearly and specifically, but not cruelly, *why*. If there is a compatibility issue, then tell them. If it is a character issue, you need to tell them that as well. "Steve, you have a lot of great qualities. I think you are really funny and kind and servant-hearted, but I have seen that you have a bad temper. I think you need to focus on that issue with God, and I want to end our courtship to allow you to do that."

Boy, oh boy, the truth hurts. Steve, in this situation, is forced to see his problem. And he is forced to admit that his temper has ended his courtship. *That* is the kind of truth in love that God uses to transform people.[2] And because of how this girl said it, Steve has the opportunity to make his *primary* relationship with *God* right.

So, what if Steve changes? What if his temper gets a million times better? Would it be possible for him and the girl to start courting again? I don't see why not. At any point, if he seems to be a good match for her, and it could result in a healthy marriage, then courting again would be a great blessing, indeed. I wouldn't advise the girl to "wait around" for that to happen—he may *never* change! But if things work out and they get back together, there is certainly nothing wrong with that.

The second thing that might happen in a courtship is that you start actually considering marriage. What does "shooting it straight" look like in that situation? The answer partly lies in this fact: there is a difference between complete transparency and complete honesty. Let me share a short little story about a friend of mine who was courting a girl and starting to get closer to proposing. As my friend went through the process of making his decision, he wanted to be completely transparent with his courtship partner. Every time he thought he was ready to propose, he would tell her. And when he was not so sure he wanted to get married to her, he would tell her that as well. He went back and forth for several weeks—a totally natural process. But it wrought havoc on this girl's emotions. It was *so hard* to hear all this back and forth! Though my friend had the best intentions, his transparency was actually a harmful policy.

Honesty in a relationship does not mean that you have to tell your courtship partner everything that's true, it means everything

2. See Ephesians 4:15; 2 Corinthians 7:10

you tell your courtship partner should be true. Wisdom would say that you should wait until you *really know* before you say anything to your partner about major decisions. If you know you don't want to spend the rest of your life with them, then tell them. If you haven't decided yet, and they ask, tell them you're still praying about it. If you know that they are the one you want by your side until you die, then tell them. But, for heaven's sake, if you say you're committed to them like that, then make it official. Again, men, step into your role as her leader, ask her father for her hand, and put a ring on it. There's no honest reason why you should stop at being "married in the eyes of God." Refusing to make a marriage legally binding is nonsensical. There should be no doubt in anyone's mind that the two of you are truly *committed*—the two of you included!

Healthy honesty avoids the emotional turmoil that comes from playing games, dragging things out, and unhealthy transparency. Boaz and Ruth shot it straight. We ought to, too.

REFLECTION QUESTIONS

1. What is difficult about shooting it straight with your courtship partner? What are the blessings of doing so?
2. Do you have a tendency toward any relationship games? What is the consequence of this tendency?
3. How have you experienced transparency being a harmful policy in relationships, dating and otherwise?

20

Trusting God for the Results

So, we arrive at the book's end. You now have a biblical framework for understanding courtship and its purpose. You have seen when it is wise to enter into a courtship. You have considered the joy of singleness and the ultimate purpose for your life. You have investigated what you should look for in a courtship partner. You have seen the blessing of having God and other people help you in that search. You have considered an argument for getting married as soon as you know you want to marry a specific person. And you have explored the ways to avoid being hurt in a relationship: through healthy boundaries and through a policy of honesty. In this final chapter, I will finish with one more principle that will tie all the other ones together.

In order for a courtship to be all it can be, those involved must do what is wise and do what is right. This has been a constant theme throughout the book, and as we have seen, it is hard work! It is difficult to make the wise decision, and it is difficult to do the right thing, *especially* when it means ending (or not even starting) a relationship. In this, we have encouragement, one last time, from Boaz and Ruth, who did the right thing and trusted God for the outcome.

Throughout Boaz and Ruth's love story, we see winks of God's sovereign hand at work. In Ruth 2:3, for example, we read, "*As it turned out*, she was working in a field belonging to Boaz" (emphasis mine). Hmmm, I wonder how that happened. In Ruth 2:12, Boaz tells Ruth, "May you be richly rewarded by the Lord." How might God reward Ruth? The Hebrew word for "reward" here (*maskoret*) implies compensation matching her loss. Ruth had lost not only her husband but also the chance of having children. Perhaps her reward would be like Leah's "wages" (*sakar*, from the same root as *maskoret*) in her children.[1] As it turned out, God used Boaz to answer his own prayer, providing Ruth with both a husband and child through him.

Throughout their story, it seemed that God was guiding Boaz and Ruth toward marriage . . . but then there was this hiccup—the unfortunate reality that Boaz couldn't actually marry Ruth like he wanted to; *God's Law* was in the way. According to the Law of Moses, if a woman was in the position of needing a kinsman redeemer, the order of priority for who got to redeem her went like this: her brother-in-law, her husband's uncle, her husband's cousin, then other close clan relatives.[2] As we see in Ruth 3:12, Boaz showed integrity and honored this law by giving the opportunity to the man who had priority over him. He clearly wanted to marry Ruth, but he did the right thing and *trusted God!* Now think about this: Boaz was a single dude, hoping to marry this awesome hottie named Ruth, and all it would take to do so was ignoring this one *itty-bitty* part of God's will. "She has everything I want and everything a good wife should have, so is it that big of a deal if this *one thing* doesn't line up?" According to Boaz, yes, it was. Boaz put everything he desired on the line to *do the right thing*. "God, this relationship is yours," said Boaz in his heart. And God blessed him for it.

When the man who had first rights on Ruth decided he just couldn't marry her,[3] Boaz wasted no time. "*Everyone! You see that*

1. Genesis 30:18
2. Numbers 27:8–11; Leviticus 25:47–49
3. Ruth 4:4–6

hot mama right there? She is now off the market!"[4] God gave Boaz the desire of his heart when Boaz gave God the relationship.

As you consider and pursue courtship and marriage, remember that the relationship should always be *God's*. Do whatever the Lord calls you to do. Hold your relationship with an open palm. He will keep it there if he wants it there, but you have to trust God when he is calling you somewhere away from your courtship partner. You have to follow him and obey him and trust that he will give you this gift if it is truly his best for you.

For me, an open palm meant going to India for two months. Kylie and I had been courting for less than a month when I followed through on my call to go overseas on a mission trip. This meant that we could have no contact for eight weeks straight (according to the mission organization's policy). It was really difficult, and it caused some relationship strain when I got back. We were in two very different emotional landscapes when I touched down in Kansas City International. I was coming home as "just a friend," waiting for God to confirm the rightness of the relationship. Kylie had been preparing for a wedding. India could have been seen as a "hiccup" in the plan.

But India was pivotal for me. God grew my faith and understanding tremendously as a result. I fell in love with a people I had never engaged with before that point. My heart broke for the lost, and I grew in Christlikeness like never before in my walk. It was all for my good, and for *our* good as well. This act of following God's call helped us both mature in Christ immensely—one more gift from God before making the two of us one. I wouldn't trade India for anything, and the relational "sacrifice" was absolutely, positively *worth it*.

As I've said before, Boaz and Ruth's story ends with continued blessing. The Lord provided them with a child and made them the ancestors of both King David and Jesus himself. God had a purpose for Boaz and Ruth far beyond just a love story. Because they did it God's way, they were blessed more than they could have asked or imagined.

4. See Ruth 4:9–10

As you court, or as you stay single, trust God in all things. Do what he tells you is right or wise to do. He knows what he is doing. He will bless your path, and he will give you strength so that you can both live for him only and leave the results up to him. When you are willing to do this and willing to follow through on the wise principles of courting from his word, he will surely give you your Boaz or your Ruth. Trust him; for God, flawless matchmaking is nothing new.

REFLECTION QUESTIONS

1. Is there any way in which you need to start holding your present or future relationship with an open palm? What exactly will this look like?
2. Are there any "right things" in your life that you need to prioritize above a relationship right now? What are they?
3. Now that you have finished this book, what commitments do you want to make for present or future relationships with God, others, and courtship partners? Consider updating your Personal Workbook as needed.

Personal Workbook

MY COURTING COMMITMENTS

Check the boxes below that you want to commit to abiding by in all future courting relationships.

I will not do the following physical things with my courtship partner:

- ☐ Side hug
- ☐ Full hug
- ☐ Hold hands while praying
- ☐ Hold hands while not praying
- ☐ Sit so close that we're touching
- ☐ Kiss on the cheek
- ☐ Kiss on the lips
- ☐ Make out
- ☐ Be alone in private
- ☐ Stay up together past ___ o'clock
- ☐ Be horizontal
- ☐ Touch intimately

I will not do the following emotional things with my courtship partner:

- ☐ Pay for their meals
- ☐ Text/call while I'm spending time with others
- ☐ Text/call after ___ o'clock
- ☐ Go on a trip together with friends
- ☐ Go on a trip together with family
- ☐ Share deep personal secrets
- ☐ Say "I love you"
- ☐ Use pet names ("Babe," "Sweetheart," etc.)

- ☐ Celebrate "anniversaries"
- ☐ Make life plans
- ☐ Name future children
- ☐ Joint-own a pet
- ☐ Share a bed

I will not do the following spiritual things with my courtship partner:

- ☐ Be accountability partners
- ☐ Specifically change churches for them
- ☐ Specifically change to their church class/group
- ☐ Habitually pray together

Signed: ______________________________ *Date:* __________

MY "LIST OF FIFTY-SEVEN"

Below, make a list of all the qualities you desire in a future spouse. You may decide to write this in letter form (with a date) as Kylie originally did.

Non-negotiables

-
-
-
-
-
-
-
-
-
-
-
-
-
-
-
-
-
-
-
-
-
-
-
-

Negotiables

-
-
-
-
-
-
-
-
-
-
-
-
-
-
-
-
-
-
-
-
-
-
-
-
-

Signed: ______________________________

Date: __________

MY LIST OF BIBLE PASSAGES

Below, record any helpful insights about manhood, womanhood, dating, or marriage that you get from your personal study of the Bible.

Passage: ____________________
Insight: ____________________

____

____

____

____

Passage: ____________________
Insight: ____________________

____

____

____

____

Passage: ____________________
Insight: ____________________

____

____

____

____

Passage: ____________________
Insight: ____________________

____

____

____

____

Passage: ______________________________

Insight: ______________________________

____

____

____

____

Passage: ______________________________

Insight: ______________________________

____

____

____

____

Passage: ______________________________

Insight: ______________________________

____

____

____

____

Passage: ______________________________

Insight: ______________________________

____

____

____

____

Passage: ______________________________

Insight: ______________________________

____

____

____

____

Passage: ____

Insight: ____

Passage: ____

Insight: ____

Passage: ____

Insight: ____

Passage: ____

Insight: ____

Bibliography

Alpert, Joseph S. "Philematology: The Science of Kissing. A Message for the Marital Month of June." *The American Journal of Medicine* 126 no. 6 (2013): 466.

Baratta, Maria. "Why You Date Someone." *Psychology Today*, Sussex, December 6, 2012.

Birth, Allyssa. "First Time for Everything: When Should Kids Get a Job, a Phone, a Date?" *The Harris Poll*, September 1, 2016.

Boyer, J. "New Name, Same Harm: Rebranding of Federal Abstinence-Only Programs." *Guttmacher Policy Review*, 21 (2018), 11–16

Brown, Anna. "Nearly Half of U.S. Adults Say Dating Has Gotten Harder for Most People in the Last 10 Years." *Pew Research Center*. August 20, 2020. https://www.pewresearch.org/social-trends/2020/08/20/nearly-half-of-u-s-adults-say-dating-has-gotten-harder-for-most-people-in-the-last-10-years/.

Bühler, Janina Larissa, Samantha Krauss, and Ulrich Orth. "Development of Relationship Satisfaction across the Life Span: A Systematic Review and Meta-Analysis." *Psychological Bulletin* 147, no. 10 (2021): 1012.

Caffin, B. C. *Commentary on 1 Peter*. In *The Pulpit Commentary*, edited by H. D. M. SpenceJones and Joseph S. Exell. London: Funk & Wagnalls Co., 1907.

Coan, James A., Hillary S. Schaefer, and Richard J. Davidson. "Lending a Hand: Social Regulation of the Neural Response to Threat." *Psychological Science* 17, no. 12 (2006): 1032–1039.

Esch, Tobias, and George B. Stefano. "The Neurobiology of Love." *Neuroendocrinology Letters* 26, no. 3 (2005): 175–92.

ESV Study Bible: English Standard Version. Wheaton, IL: Crossway, 2007.

"Figure MS-2: Median Age at First Marriage: 1890 to Present." *United States Census Bureau*, 2020.

Gallace, Alberto, and Charles Spence. "The Science of Interpersonal Touch: An Overview." *Neuroscience & Biobehavioral Reviews* 34, no. 2 (2010): 246–59.

Han, Yixue, et al. "A Decade of Love: Mapping the Landscape of Romantic Love Research through Bibliometric Analysis." *Humanities and Social Sciences Communications* 11, no. 1 (2024): 1–16.

Hanzal, Alesia, Chris Segrin, and Sybilla M. Dorros. "The Role of Marital Status and Age on Men's and Women's Reactions to Touch from a Relational Partner." *Journal of Nonverbal Behavior* 32, no. 1 (2008): 21–35.

Jones, David W. "Divorce and Remarriage." *Bibliotheca sacra* 165 (2008): 68–85.

Keener, Craig S, and John H. Walton. *NKJV Cultural Backgrounds Study Bible: Bringing to Life the Ancient World of Scripture.* Grand Rapids, MI: Zondervan, 2017.

Meier, Ann, and Gina Allen. "Romantic Relationships from Adolescence to Young Adulthood: Evidence from the National Longitudinal Study of Adolescent Health." *The Sociological Quarterly* 50, no. 2 (2009): 308–35.

Ogan, Matthew A., et al. "The Role of Emotional Dysregulation in the Association between Family-of-Origin Conflict and Romantic Relationship Maintenance." *Journal of Marital and Family Therapy* 50, no. 1 (2024): 28–44.

Regan, Pamela C., et al. "Gender, Ethnicity, and the Developmental Timing of First Sexual and Romantic Experiences." *Social Behavior and Personality* 32, no. 7 (2004): 667–76.

Seraj, Sarah, Kate G. Blackburn, and James W. Pennebaker. "Language Left Behind on Social Media Exposes the Emotional and Cognitive Costs of a Romantic Breakup." *Proceedings of the National Academy of Sciences* 118, no. 7 (2021): e2017154118

Smalley, Greg. "Eight Great Reasons to Date." *CBN.com*, October 1, 2019.

STD Surveillance Network. "SSuN Special Focus Report: Age of First Sexual Intercourse." *Virginia Department of Health*, October 2012.

Wang, Wendy, and Kim Parker. "Record Share of Americans Have Never Married." *Pew Research Center*, September 24, 2014. https://www.pewresearch.org/social-trends/2014/09/24/record-share-of-americans-have-never-married/.

Wlodarski, Rafael, and Robin IM Dunbar. "Examining the Possible Functions of Kissing in Romantic Relationships." *Archives of Sexual Behavior* 42, no. 8 (2013): 1415–1423.

Yarnell, Jason. "Biblical Manhood Study." Lecture, 2016.

www.ingramcontent.com/pod-product-compliance
Lightning Source LLC
LaVergne TN
LVHW050650100826
845148LV00011B/2055

* 9 7 9 8 3 8 5 2 7 1 8 0 1 *